SNAILS
of land and sea

SNAILS
of land and sea

Hilda Simon

Illustrated by the author

The VANGUARD PRESS · New York

Contents

List of Illustrations

SNAILS
of land and sea

Snails in the History of Man

Many people who enjoy the pastime of collecting shells along the seashore, admiring their diverse shapes and handsome patterns, are unaware of the animals housed in those shells during their lifetime. As a matter of fact, most amateur collectors would be quite surprised to discover that a large percentage of the shells they find are snail shells.

It seems rather strange that the habits and lifestyles of both the terrestrial and marine snails should be so little known, considering their importance to man throughout his history. Since ancient times, snails have been used by people around the world in a variety of ways—as food and currency, for dyes, jewelry, and artifacts—ways that made them significant factors in the cultural and economic affairs of many regions. There is evidence that snails were eaten by prehistoric man, and even today they are important food items in certain countries. On the negative side, some species inflict heavy damage on human food sources both on the land and in the sea, and others pose health hazards by harboring dangerous parasites.

Despite the impact of these animals on many different areas of human life, traditionally it was the empty shell left after the death of the animal it housed that received the lion's share of attention, whereas the snail that produced and owned the shell was largely ignored. Only the edible snails, and those used for purposes requiring parts of the animal other than the shell, became somewhat better known, at least to the people who captured them for profit.

Shell collecting, on the other hand, is probably the oldest of all human hobbies. At a number of ancient sites archaeologists have unearthed shells that undoubtedly served only as ornaments, including species not indigenous to the regions in which they were found. For example, exotic shells from the Indian and Pacific Oceans were recovered in France from caves that had been inhabited by the Cro-Magnons, who flourished 30,-000 years ago. This fascinating breed of tall people, with a skull shaped strikingly like that of modern man, is famed for the fine paintings of animals found on these cave walls. The presence of exotic shells in their caves would indicate that some kind of trading activity linking Europe and the Far East existed before the ancient civilizations.

Not quite so old, but predating the construction of the Egyptian pyramids by several centuries, are the collections of shells found in many archaeological sites of both the Old and New Worlds, which also include tropical species from faraway regions, presumably treasured as objects of trade.

In ancient Greece Aristotle is believed to have possessed a sizeable collection of shells. However, the most famous snails of those times in the Mediterranean countries were sought neither for their shells nor for their meat, but for a peculiar small gland located near their gills. This gland provided the ancient cultures with the most coveted pigment ever sought by man: the precious "imperial purple" dye. The Latin word for the pigment-yielding snail was *purpura,* which comes from the Greek *porphyra;* the importance of this color in ancient times is indicated by such designations as *purpurati,* the "purple-robed" elite of Rome. It has come down to us not only in our word "purple" but also in the expression "born to the purple," meaning born to a high station in life.

Snails of two closely related genera, the more important of which is the widely distributed Murex group, yield the pigment prized so highly in those days. A deep, somewhat reddish violet, its hue may vary somewhat with the species as well as with the region in which the snails are found. The more reddish the hue, the more precious the dye became, especially in the first decades of the Christian era. One Roman writes that the violet

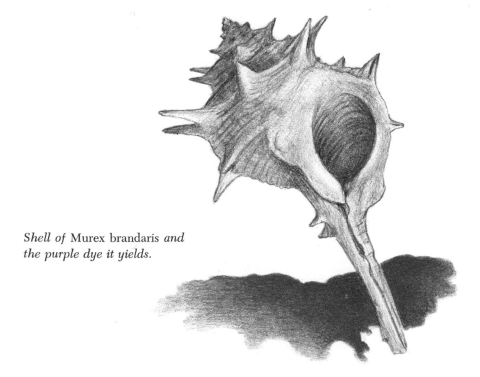

Shell of Murex brandaris *and the purple dye it yields.*

purple costing a hundred *denarii* per pound was the fashion in his youth, but that later the "double purple" from Phoenicia, at a thousand *denarii* a pound, became the rage. Undoubtedly this preference for the more reddish hues inspired the cleverest among the old masters of the art of dyeing to use every trick of the trade to get the desired shade.

Production centers for the precious dye were scattered throughout the entire Mediterranean region. One famous site was the city of Tyre in Phoenicia, which, as we just mentioned, evidently yielded a naturally reddish purple dye; the largest probably existed in Rome, where the shells of the snails used in extracting the dye were piled up in huge mounds, the famous *Monte testaceo* being one of these artificial shell hills.

Later, the costly and difficult process of dye production from snail glands was discarded as other pigments began to be substituted for the original purple. From that time on, the designation "purple" was increasingly used for a wide variety of red shades including crimson, a color that replaced the traditional reddish-violet purple for the robes of royalty in many European countries.

Another group of snails greatly prized in the past were the cowries; these, however, were coveted strictly for the beauty of their highly polished shells. In Germany, the popular name of this group is porcelain snails, and their shells are widely known as porcelain shells to European collectors. The English word "porcelain" today is identified with fine chinaware, but it originally comes from *porcellana*, the Italian name of the Venus cowrie.

How widely the shells of these snails were used as currency is evident in both the popular and scientific names of at least one species, the money cowrie, *Cypraea moneta*, perhaps the most commercially important of all the cowries in certain parts

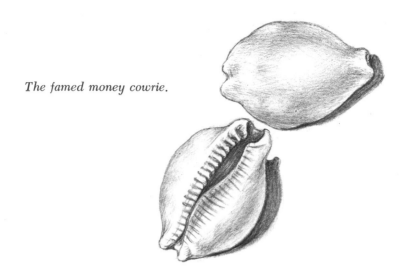

The famed money cowrie.

of the world. For hundreds of years, cowrie shells by the ton were shipped from Ceylon and other ports of the Indian Ocean to Africa, and especially to Zanzibar, where they were traded inland. In some of the independent states of Central Africa, the income of black African rulers was counted in cowrie shells rather than in precious metals or other valuables, and much of the slave trade within Africa was paid for in the same currency. Thus one European traveler reported in the early eighteenth century that Arab slave traders paid a total of 12,000 pounds of cowrie shells to a Negro ruler for six hundred slaves he had captured during a raid on a neighboring tribe. Based upon that rate, an individual slave was worth about twenty pounds of cowrie shells at that time. However, inflation soon set in as cowrie shells in unprecedented numbers were dumped on the African market, and fifty years later the shell money had been drastically devalued, and other items began to replace it.

The shell money of the North American Indians consisted mainly of the famous wampum, beads made from clam shells and often fashioned into belts. However, the peculiar tooth, or

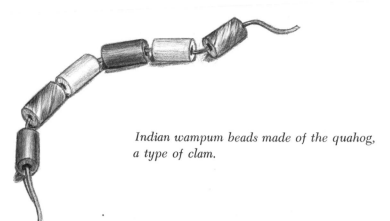

*Indian wampum beads made of the quahog,
a type of clam.*

tusk, shells, so called because they look like miniature elephants' tusks, also were popular both as currency and as highly prized ornaments. The Indians used many other types of shells, including cowries, in their ornamental artifacts; one of their favorites was the huge Pacific marine snail, the abalone. Beautifully iridescent on the inside, the shells of these large snails have long been used to make very attractive jewelry. For centuries, abalone shells were traded widely inland by the tribes along the Pacific coast. The abalone is one of the relatively few snails hunted both for its delicious meat and for its beautiful shell—a combination that all but wiped out the abalone population on the California coast in the early years of this century. At that time, entire fleets of Japanese fishing boats anchored offshore while their crews ravaged almost to extinction the abalone colonies along the coast near Mexico. Only after in-

Silver pillbox inlaid with abalone shell.

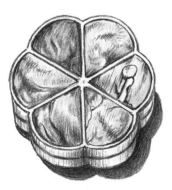

Live tooth shell with the animal protruding from it.

censed Californians pressed for measures prohibiting this type of abuse did the large snails begin to make a comeback.

Individual snail shells prized for their beauty have been important to a variety of people in different countries. Thus, in Korea, only the bravest of brave warriors were permitted to wear, as a special ornament in the hair or around the neck, the shells of the egg snail, so called because of its shape. This snail is a large and handsome relative of the cowries. In Europe, on the other hand, the shells of a group called cone snails were in great demand and brought the highest prices among collectors, who are known to have paid fabulous sums for certain rare specimens. In 1766, the mayor of the Dutch city of Delft was the proud owner of a shell called the "orange admiral," a rare cone for which he refused offers of several hundred guilders. Although the comparative value of the old Dutch guilder, which was a gold coin, is difficult to establish in terms of modern currencies, the sums offered were high by any standards.

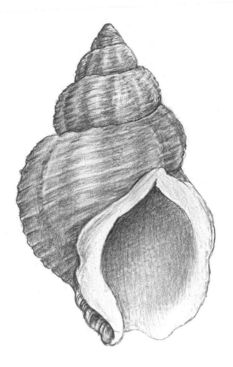

One of the common edible whelks.

Even today, a rare shell may bring up to several hundred dollars among collecting enthusiasts, who pursue their fascinating hobby as avidly as any stamp or coin collector.

Of equal but of much more common importance were the edible snails of both land and ocean, and a number of these species still are staple food items in many regions of the world. A group of large marine snails widely used for food, especially in Europe, are the whelks. The meat of the abalone, already mentioned, is very tasty when properly prepared, and the famous *escargots,* the terrestrial edible snails, known especially as a French delicacy, are shipped from France all over the world.

Important to man in a much less pleasant way are those snails that destroy certain crops or animals used as food by humans. North America has relatively few native terrestrial pest species, but there are a number of carnivorous marine snails, such as the oyster drills, that prey on, and occasionally take a heavy toll of, economically important mollusks including oysters and clams. In Europe and Africa, certain terrestrial snails may do considerable damage to seedling grain, lettuce,

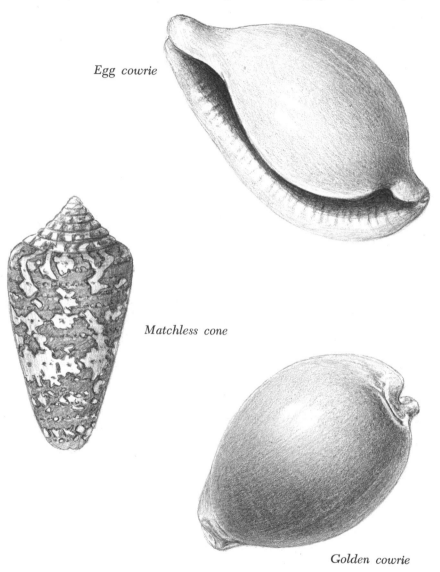

Egg cowrie

Matchless cone

Golden cowrie

Shell of the edible snail Helix pomatica.

and other crops; the African giant snail, accidently imported into the United States, has become an agricultural pest in Florida.

In Africa, the most serious threat posed by snails is the involuntary role played by certain fresh-water species that are intermediary hosts to the larvae of dangerous parasites. The trematode worm *Bilharzia haematobia,* for instance, is one of man's most feared parasites. The complex development of this worm begins when its free-swimming larvae enter fresh-water snails, and later leave these intermediate hosts to atack any large vertebrate, including man, that swims, bathes in, or drinks from, lakes or streams inhabited by these snails. Entering the warm-blooded host's body through the skin or by way of the mouth, the worms eventually settle in the large veins of the pelvic region and the urinary tract, causing painful and debilitating disorders that may lead to death unless treated in

Liver fluke and its intermediary host,
a common fresh-water snail.

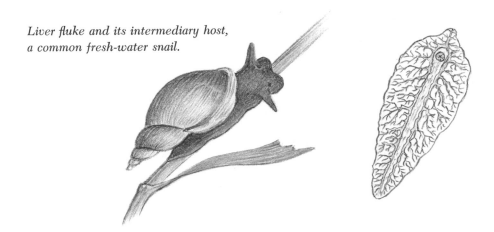

time. Attempts to control the worms through large-scale attacks on the host snails have been only partially successful.

In the pages that follow, we shall meet all the snails mentioned here and many others—the beautiful and the homely, the beneficial and the harmful, the vegetarians and the predators, the tree climbers and those that live on the ocean floor.

Evolution and Anatomy

The most tantalizing questions·about the early stages of evolution arise from the absence of a clear fossil record. Although it must be assumed that a varied and abundant animal life existed in those primordial oceans of almost a billion years ago, the soft bodies of the ancient creatures decayed and disappeared after death without leaving behind distinct outlines from which their shapes and sizes can be determined. The earliest fossils found in large numbers date from the Cambrian period, which began about five hundred million years ago and lasted for approximately one hundred million years. During that period many animals developed hard, protective sheaths or shells that remained intact long after their death and the disintegration of the soft parts of their bodies, and thus left lasting impressions in the mud and silt of the ocean floor.

From that time about 400 million years ago up to and including the present, the mollusks—animals with soft, unsegmented

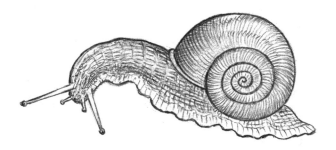

Drawing of a snail in a French zoological work of 1551.

bodies usually protected by calcareous shells—have thrived. To-day, they make up the large phylum of Mollusca, comprising about 55,000 living, and at least as many extinct, fossil kinds. One of the primary divisions of the animal and plant kingdoms, each phylum is divided into classes, and the classes into successively smaller categories, ending with the species, the most narrowly defined group of related plants or animals.

Until quite recently, the phylum of mollusks had five classes. A few decades ago, however, a sixth was added when a group of primitive mollusks was "promoted" from an order to a class. A seventh class, consisting of only five species, joined the group in 1958, when first one, and shortly afterward four more species believed to have been extinct for some 300 million years were dredged up from deep waters; these five mollusks are truly "in a class by themselves."

Under present designation, the most primitive class of mollusks are peculiar worm-like creatures known as solenogasters; they are followed by the chitons, which look somewhat like the familiar "pillbugs." Then come the gastroverms, the newly discovered "living fossils." The fourth class, comprising all the snails and slugs, is also the largest, with more than 37,000 species. The tooth shells make up the fifth class; the sixth—oysters, clams, and their kin—are a large group of some 15,000 species. Finally, there is number seven: the squids and octopuses, not very numerous but the most advanced of all mollusks. It is interesting to note that the two large classes account for more than 95 percent—the snails and slugs alone for over 65 percent—of all living mollusks.

Snails and other types of mollusks that were plentiful in the Cambrian period are believed to have evolved from certain wormlike ancestors in pre-Cambrian times, and then to have branched out into a variety of different groups. Fossils of ancient snails indicate that they, and quite probably also the animals once housed in them, were surprisingly similar to some of the snails living today.

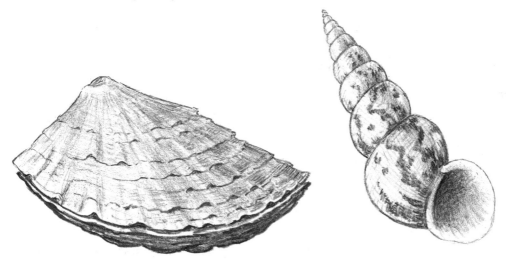

Bivalve (oyster) and univalve (snail) shells.

If, as mentioned earlier, many amateur collectors find it somewhat difficult to distinguish between the various types of shell-bearing invertebrates, they can take comfort in the fact that different groups such as snails, clams, and even barnacles, which, despite their appearance, are crustaceans, were confused by early zoologists, and that beginning students today also frequently find themselves in the same predicament. After all, we must not forget that the phylum Mollusca comprises fully as many species as all the five classes of vertebrates from fish to mammals taken together.

Snails and slugs make up the class known as Gastropoda, from the Greek words *gaster*, meaning belly, and *podos*, foot. The gastropods are distinguished from clams, oysters, and similar mollusks by the distinct, tentacle-equipped head, and the long, ventral foot that enables them to move. In addition, the majority of species has a single unchambered shell, which makes them *univalves*, in contrast to *bivalves* such as clams, which have a hinged two-part shell. There are also many shell-less gastropods, and two peculiar bivalve snails.

The gastropods are divided into several subclasses, which are further subdivided into orders and families of varying sizes. All these groups, shell-bearing and shell-less alike, share certain anatomical features, such as a distinct head, tentacles, and a well-developed gastrointestinal system, which, along with the other internal organs, is rotated, or coiled, to 180 degrees. Otherwise, there exist many modifications of the soft parts, and an enormous variety of shell form and pattern in the different species. Thus mouth parts, shape and size of the tentacles, size of foot and mantle, and type of breathing organs may vary even among closely related groups. Similarly, the shell may be long or short; formed like a cap, a cone, or a spindle; colored solidly from white to almost black, or patterned in every conceivable

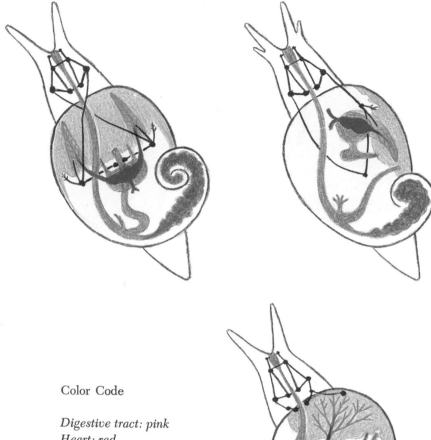

Color Code

Digestive tract: pink
Heart: red
Gills (lung): blue
Kidney: brown
Liver: purple
Mantle: yellow
Mantle cavity: green
Nervous system: black

Diagram of the internal organs in three subclasses of gastropods.

Color Code

Body: tan
Digestive tract: pink
Eyes: red
Foot: purple
Genital pore: green
Head: orange
Mantle: yellow
Mantle cavity: light blue
Respiratory pore: blue
Shell: brown

Diagram of the basic anatomy of Helix pomatica.

combination of rings, spots, blotches, streaks, or stripes. The very special rules governing growth and structure of the shell will be discussed in the next chapter.

The first of the three subclasses comprises the Prosobranchia, snails whose heart is usually located behind the gills; this group includes many primitive herbivorous kinds as well as numerous carnivores, some of them highly evolved. The second subclass is called Ophistobranchia; the members of this group are distinguished by gills located behind the heart; most species also have a shell that is greatly reduced or completely internal, or may be missing altogether in the adult stage. The final subclass, the Pulmonata, includes all the terrestrial and fresh-water species that are equipped with lungs and breathe air; scientists believe these snails evolved when certain marine gastropods migrated to fresh water, and some then invaded the land to take up a terrestrial way of life. A few of the Pulmonata later returned to fresh water and again became aquatic, though they retained their lungs—a fact that forces them to surface at regular intervals if they are not to drown.

The typical snail, such as one of the "garden snails" of the genus *Helix,* has a fleshy head, the most conspicuous feature of which is the longer of the two pairs of tentacles that bear the eyes. All four tentacles can be completely retracted. Although the eyes have a cornea, lens, and retina, the vision of a typical snail is not very good, and it is believed many snails are not capable of distinguishing more than shadows and light. The mouth is equipped with a horny jaw and a file-like tongue called the radula. In many marine species, the mouth parts can be protruded to form a long proboscis. On the right side of the head just behind the tentacles is the opening of the genital pore.

The head is joined directly to the large muscular foot, which bears the shell. Both the horny, organic matter and the inorganic limy deposits that create the shell are secreted by glands in the mantle, a thin membrane that lines the shell and sur-

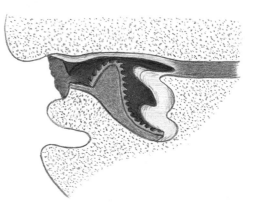

Color Code

Esophagus: orange
Mouth: purple
Muscles: yellow
Radula: pink
Teeth: green

Diagram of the mouthparts of a snail.

Land snail laying eggs in a nest prepared in the soil.

rounds the internal organs. At the edge of the shell in the front are the comparatively large respiratory pore and, right beside it, the much smaller anal opening in the mantle margin. Through action of the large columella muscle, which extends internally to the spire at the top of the shell, the snail's soft parts can be drawn completely into the shell.

The internal organs include a heart, lung—replaced by gills in almost all marine, and some fresh-water, species—a single kidney, a liver, and the reproductive system. The sexes are separate in most marine snails, and reproduction is normal, the female laying the eggs after fertilization by the male. All pulmonate snails, however, are hermaphrodites, combining male and female sexual organs in each individual. The reproduction of these snails is preceded by a courtship and during the mating performance each partner fertilizes the eggs of the other by inserting a copulatory organ into the genital pore on the head, and so transferring the sperm. Each snail then deposits its batch of eggs, covered by a jelly-like substance, from which many days later the young, already equipped with shells and looking like miniature adults, emerge to take up the way of life of their particular species.

Most marine gastropods go through a different development, a development that includes a free-swimming larval stage called a veliger (from the velum, a veil-like swimming organ), and only later do these gastropods metamorphose into the typical adult snail. Marine snails usually produce huge numbers of eggs to compensate for depredations by their many natural enemies.

Biologically a highly successful group, snails survived even as more advanced animals evolved, and they spread throughout the world to almost every habitat that can sustain life. They occur from the tropics to the subpolar regions; they have been found at depths of 17,000 feet in the ocean, and at altitudes of up to 18,000 feet in the Himalayan mountains. Although basically creatures of the water, some land snails have adapted so well to semi-arid conditions that they can survive in certain desert areas. As a rule, however, land snails are most numerous in damp, moist localities, and appear especially after rain. If exposed to dryness for any length of time without protection, a snail will die quickly. Keeping a shell-less slug in a box without moisture for twenty-four hours will inevitably result in the animal's death. Land snails with shells, on the other hand, can protect themselves efficiently against dehydration by withdrawing into their shells and closing off the aperture with a tempo-

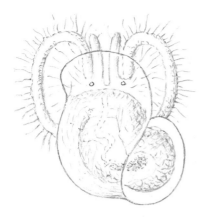

Almost transparent veliger larva of a worm snail.

rary covering called an epiphragm, which consists of mucus and lime hardened into a tough membrane. In this manner, snails can survive in hot, dry climates, "summering" inside their shells throughout the dry season until the rains come again and they awaken to new life.

The shell also offers some protection against certain enemies, although the majority of snail-eating animals, which include other snails, crabs, birds, and mammals, are deterred neither by the shell nor by the mucous slime usually covering the soft parts. As a matter of fact, there are several kinds of birds that feed predominantly or even exclusively on snails, such as the limpkins of the Southeastern United States and parts of Central and South America. The most specialized of all is the rare Everglade kite, a bird of prey that lives entirely on a single species of fresh-water snail. Its bill ends in a long, thin, sharply curved point, which it uses to pull the snails from their shells. However, mammals ranging from dormice to racoons also consider snails as much of a delicacy as do some humans. High on the list of smaller enemies against which the shell offers no protection are the larvae of fireflies, which live almost exclusively on snails and slugs.

If desiccation is no problem for marine snails, a host of enemies, numbering many times those besetting their terrestrial cousins, makes survival precarious for the salt-water species. Their shells, which are often thick and hard, offer some protection, and the operculum, a horny or calcareous plate on the foot of most marine gastropods, can efficiently close off the opening of the shell. As in the case of land snails, however, shells are at best a flimsy protection against numerous predators ranging from crabs to fish and humans, all of which share a liking for tasty gastropods. Some marine snails have developed weapons such as poisonous stings—or rather bites—that have the double function of helping to capture prey and warding off attacks by enemies. Especially the shell-less snails, or slugs, both on land and sea, have evolved a variety of defenses ranging from copious and often ill-tasting secretions to a unique and complicated method of assimilating and using the poison-dart weapons of marine creatures, such as sea anemones, after first eating the owners of these weapons. By and large, however, marine gastropods have to rely on their powers of reproduction and the huge numbers of eggs they produce for the survival of their kind.

The large, hard, spiral operculum of a sea snail.

Color Code

Body: Brown
Eyes: blue
Mantle: pink
Operculum: green
Shell: yellow
Siphon: orange

Diagram of the main body parts of a sea snail.

The number of species as well as the diversity in appearance and habits is much greater among the marine snails than among those that live on land. This diversity is strikingly apparent in shell forms and patterns; less well-known is the fact that this variation applies equally to the animals occupying the shells during their lifetime. Thus the body of a marine snail may be so small that the shell hides it completely, or so large that it protrudes on all sides and appears much too big to be withdrawn into the shell. Similarly, size and shape of feelers and mouth parts vary greatly, as does the mantle, which may be enlarged into lateral lobes that all but envelop the shell or modified to form a siphon, or breathing tube.

Marine snails occur in practically all parts of the ocean. Some are pelagic, which means they are found far from the shore, swimming about in the open sea, or living out their life in floating seaweed. Others prefer the shallow waters of coastal regions and are often found in tidal pools. Still others occur at great depths where there is little other marine life. A few lead a more or less fixed, stationary existence; many are active prowlers of the ocean floor. Their food preferences may range from seaweed to other snails and fish. Whatever the individual species' method of adaptation and survival, it has been eminently successful in all cases, except when man has intervened to destroy the natural balance of the snails' environment.

In the chapters that follow, representatives of the various large groups of gastropods will be shown and discussed in an attempt to illustrate the wealth of diversity of appearance, habits, and behavior patterns that distinguish this large and interesting class of mollusks.

Growth and Structure
of the Shell

The bewildering variety of gastropod shell shapes and patterns makes it difficult to believe that there is a single basic architectural blueprint for all those different-looking forms, yet such a blueprint does exist. From the flat, cap-like shapes of some snail shells to the steeply pointed spires, the grotesquely jagged silhouettes, or smooth, egg-shaped outlines of others, all of them are based upon, and begin with, the same simple spiral structure in the embryo snail.

This structure is externally clearly visible in the shells of land snails, as well as in those of a great many marine gastropods. In most instances, the spiral is coiled clockwise when seen from above looking at the apex of the shell; such shells are called right-handed, or dextral. The exceptions are the left-handed, or sinistral, shells in which the spiral coils counter-clockwise. No one knows why these few species are different from the rule applying to the majority.

Right-handed (dextral) shell.

Left-handed (sinistral) shell.

The internal structure of the shell can easily be observed by slicing a shell in half from top to its opening. Even more instructive are the beautiful, clear pictures produced by X-rays of the undamaged shell, showing it to be an elongated cone wound around an axis, called the columella, to which are attached, during the lifetime of the animal, the muscles that permit the snail to withdraw all its soft parts into the shell.

In the majority of species, the individual whorls are marked by suture lines; each successive whorl partially covers the preceding, smaller, one. The largest whorl has the opening, called the aperture, through which the animal can protrude its head and foot during periods of activity. After withdrawal into its

Horizontal cut through a snail shell.

shell, a land snail can close off the aperture with its epiphragm, and in most marine gastropods the shell opening can be closed by the operculum.

The small whorls at the apex of the shell, which in marine species represent the shell of the free-swimming larval form, may differ considerably from those added later by the mature animal. Thus shells of the genus *Murex* and other marine snails feature projections, spines, and ribs completely lacking in the larval portion of the shell. Other species of both marine and land snails continue to add whorls identical to the early ones in everything except size as they grow and mature.

The shell of gastropods consists typically of two different components: an outer, organic framework of horny matter

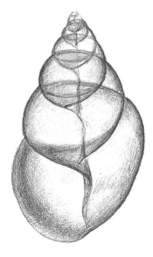

X-ray picture of a tree-snail shell.

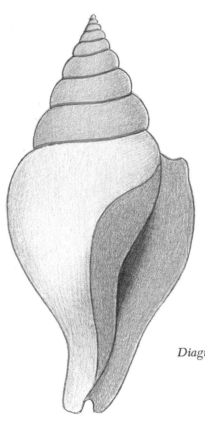

Color Code

Aperture: red
Body whorl: yellow
Inner lip: orange
Outer lip: pink
Spire: green
Suture lines: blue

Diagram of major shell parts.

called the periostracum, and three inner-structured layers of inorganic calcareous material. The outer "skin" is made of a hardened protein called conchiolin. In many older shells, much of this is naturally eroded. Shell collectors usually remove the rest and polish the shell to bring out the full strength of the colors of the calcareous layers beneath the periostracum. Some gastropods, especially those whose shell is normally covered and protected by the mantle during their lifetime, do not have a periostracum.

The calcium carbonates of the inner layers are secreted by the mantle, and deposited in thin plates or leaf-like crystals in two different crystalline forms, often interspersed with platelets of conchiolin. In shells displaying the iridescent rainbow colors, the thin plates of the nacreous surface layers are arranged in a special structure spacing them at regular distances. This causes certain light waves to be refracted and reinforced, and others to be absorbed, resulting in the appearance of the so-called colors of thin films, the pure rainbow hues of the spectrum. This phenomenon was first described by Robert Boyle, a contemporary of Sir Isaac Newton, and serves as an explanation of all the pure colors produced by thin films such as soap bubbles, oil slicks, or—in their more permanent form—iridescent beetle wings, and the nacre of mollusk shells. All these colors are an exclusive product of light refracted by special tissue structures and are therefore called structural colors.

Although all the pearly, iridescent, hues are produced by light refraction only, and are independent of pigmentation, the majority of shell colors result from pigments deposited along with the calcareous material by the snail's mantle as the shell grows. Most of these pigments belong to just two large groups: the melanins, comprising all hues from tan to brown and black, and the carotenoids, the yellow and orange shades. Some red porphyrins also occur, and there are isolated instances of blue and violet pigments, although the blue and green hues found in shells are usually those produced by light refraction; but then most blue and green shades in the animal world are structural rather than pigmental. From the bright blue of a feather

Color Code

Center Layers: yellow, pink
Inner layer: blue
Periostracum: green

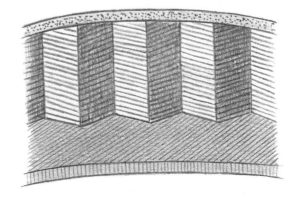

Diagram of shell structure.

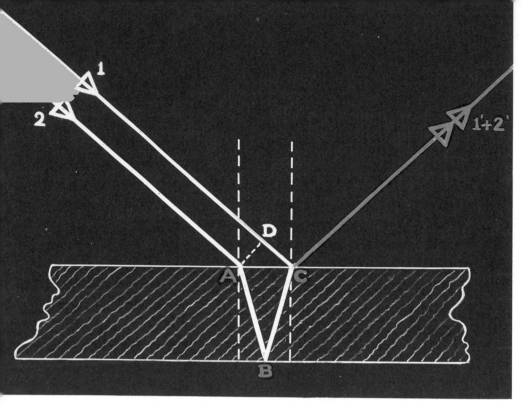

Diagram of light interference. By passing through thin films, and being reflected at the lower surfaces, white light is separated into its component colors, which then appear as pure, non-pigment, mother-of-pearl or rainbow hues.

to that of a fish scale, the majority of these colors result from light refraction rather than blue pigment. Similarly, green is usually a combination of structural blue and pigmental yellow, although exceptions confirm the rule here as everywhere else.

The general lack of green and blue shades among shells is compensated for by the wide range of other hues. Pure white, cream, and gray; every shade of yellow, pink, and orange; browns from tan to chestnut and cinnamon; fiery reds and shiny blacks—all these shades are represented, and often combined, in an endless variety of patterns that challenge the imagination. In addition, a highly glazed surface may enhance, and a sculptured one subtly change, the prevailing color scheme.

By and large, the rule applies that the brightest shell colors are found in tropical waters and that the hues are progressively paler the farther one gets away from the equator. Shells found in arctic waters are usually almost completely white or gray. This, of course, conforms to the general pattern, found in both plant and animal life, of brilliant colors and luxurious growth in the tropical zones far surpassing that of the cooler regions.

One of the great mysteries of shell development is the mechanism in the genetic code that produces the individual shapes and colors of each species in a system finely regulated to deposit both shell material and pigment in a specific pattern. All color patterns found in shells are based upon one or more of four pigment-deposit rhythms. Perhaps the simplest is the one that deposits the pigment continuously over the entire width of the growth area, which results in a solid-colored shell. If pigment is deposited continuously, but only in localized zones of the growth area, the shell will eventually display a pattern of longitudinal stripes. Pigment deposited over the entire width of the area but discontinuously, only at regular intervals, produces horizontal stripes. And, finally, pigment deposits limited to localized zones *and* spaced at intervals create a pattern of spots or blotches. The last-mentioned pattern may appear in the form of colorless spots on a colored background if the pigmented zones are large compared with the pigment-free areas,

Unpolished and two polished specimens of the giant buttontop, a tropical top shell. Many shells have such normally invisible mother-of-pearl layers.

Four different types of pigment deposit patterns in shells.

or it may show colored spots on a colorless background if the reverse is true. Modifications of these deposit rhythms are responsible for the entire vast array of different shell patterns.

A very similar process of varying shell-material deposits at regular intervals produces the sculptured surfaces of many shells. Highly specialized deposit patterns create some of the unusual shell forms, including those with bizarre projections, as well as the smooth egg-shaped shells, in which the spire is completely embedded and no longer visible from the outside.

As in the case of many other animal patterns, those of mollusk shells have confronted scientists with the problem of explaining why a considerable portion of the genetic code that directs the overall development of the organism is being devoted to create variations in adornment and appearance. Many biologists have considered such apparently nonessential patterns simply as byproducts of other functions vital to the survival of the animal. This view was strengthened, temporarily at least, by the discovery that some colors in the surface tissues of certain mollusks are indeed waste products. Moreover, according to present evolutionary theory, colors that cannot now be traced directly to the elimination of waste products, as well as shapes and symmetry of the patterns themselves, might have originated as byproducts of an animal's metabolism and later acquired functional importance for the survival of the species by natural selection.

These views, however, have come increasingly under fire by biologists who find such explanations unsatisfactory, especially

Three stages in the growth of a conch shell. The two immature stages lack the extravagant projections of the mature shell.

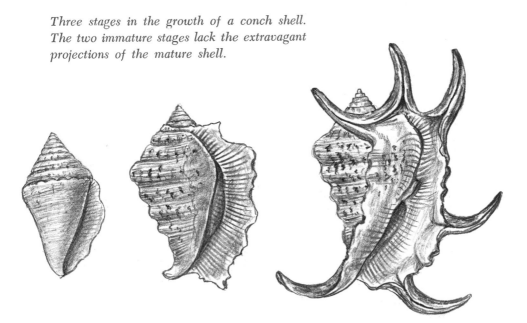

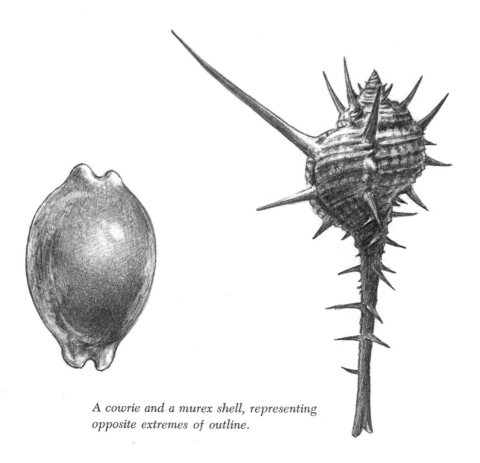

A cowrie and a murex shell, representing opposite extremes of outline.

for shell colors and patterns. They can play no role in sex recognition, for the snails themselves cannot see them, since their eyes are incapable of perceiving sophisticated images. Nor do the colors serve as a warning, since, apart from the fact that predators rarely eat the shell, many snails with bright colors are coveted food items for a number of animals. In addition, in some extremely colorful species the greatly enlarged mantle normally covers much of the shell during the snail's lifetime. Shell patterns—and many others in both the animal and plant worlds—are persuasive arguments for the claim that such "excess beauty" goes far beyond any narrow function serving mere existence or survival. Instead, the differences in appearance seem to be, according to the noted Swiss zoologist, Dr. Adolf Portmann, a kind of "self-expression" of the organism, blueprinted in the genetic code of each species to set it uniquely apart from others of its kind.

Naturalists today must accept the fact that, even as they solve many of the mysteries of functional phenomena in living beings, much of what they encounter during their research is, and probably will remain forever, beyond the scope of our understanding. This realization can only increase the wonder and enhance the enjoyment of the natural beauty on our planet, a beauty exquisitely expressed in the shapes and patterns of a great many snail shells.

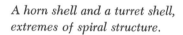

A horn shell and a turret shell, extremes of spiral structure.

Land Snails

In the minds of many people, a snail is the embodiment of deliberate slowness, crawling along at the proverbial "snail's pace" and incapable of moving quickly even if its life depends upon speed. Somehow, in the popular image of the garden snail with its stalked, retractile eyes and its single broad foot, this slowness is associated with the fact that the snail has to carry its house on its back, and is therefore unduly burdened.

The snails' rate of locomotion has nothing to do with their shell, however, for the shell-less slugs, which do not have to carry that load, move just as slowly as their shell-bearing cousins, a fact acknowledged in the term "sluggish" applied to anything or anyone slow or lazy. The snails' way of moving about is determined by the structure of the foot, and is part of a specialized lifestyle, which, despite the lack of speed, has proved highly successful.

Terrestrial snails occur mainly in the warmer regions of the world. Although North America has many hundreds of different kinds, they are usually not abundant, and—with the exception of a few accidentally introduced foreign species— none of them is economically important. In Europe, Africa, and Asia, however, numerous species of snails are abundant in many regions; some of them are economic factors either because of damage they do or because of the food they provide.

Generally, attractively colored shells are more common among marine snails than among the land snails; many of the latter have rather dull-colored brownish or grayish shells that would not win any prize for beauty. Quite a few, however, have handsomely colored and often highly glazed shells, fully as attractive as some of the collectors' favorites from the sea. One of them is the North American arboreal snail *Liguus fasciatus,* a native of Florida and one of the most beautiful land snails on this continent. Unfortunately, its continued survival has recently been threatened by the destruction of its native habitat through land development. This fact is made even more regrettable by the harmlessness of the beautiful tree climber, which feeds on lichens, mosses, and algae, but never damages any of the trees on which it lives.

One of the most intriguing facts about *Liguus* is its tendency to occur in many different color forms, or subspecies. More than fifty of such different forms have been recorded, with colors ranging from pure glazed white to a beautiful pattern of chocolate brown and golden yellow. Collectors are reported to have paid as much as fifty dollars for a single especially rare and beautiful specimen.

Despite heartwarming efforts to insure this snail's survival, it will take some time to find out whether the conservationists have been successful. If they are, the credit will be due to the

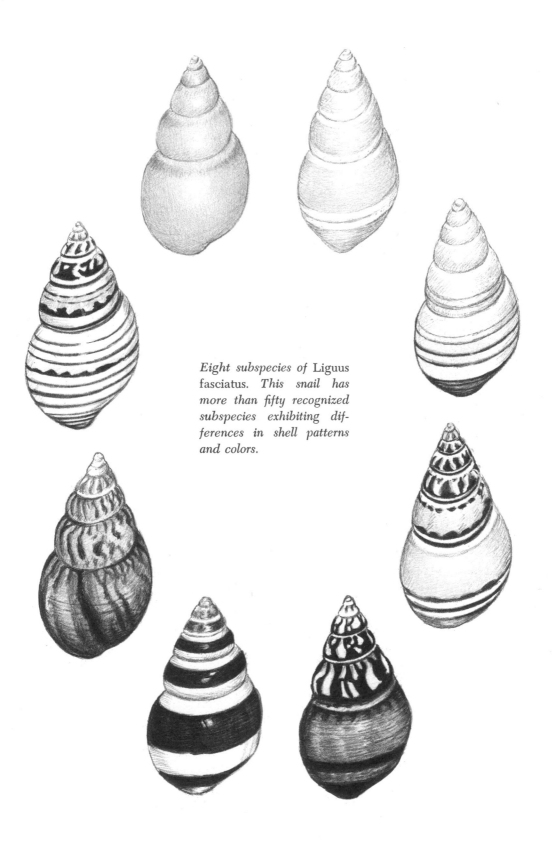

Eight subspecies of Liguus fasciatus. This snail has more than fifty recognized subspecies exhibiting differences in shell patterns and colors.

businessmen, National Parks rangers, biologists, and other ad-
mirers of this snail's beauty who banded together to map a
feasible strategy.

The main difficulty lay in the fact that the snail can live only
in the hammock-soil environment of certain parts of Florida,
which extensive drainage for land development has changed
completely, endangering a number of other animals along with
the handsome tree snail.

In order to save the snail from extinction, the conservationists
began transplanting small colonies into suitable areas of the
Everglades National Park, where the snails, along with other
wildlife, would be safe from further encroachment by man. So
far, the venture seems to be successful; although the handsome
creatures have disappeared forever from their home ranges in
the Miami-Fort Lauderdale-Pompano Beach areas, many have
taken to their new home grounds in the Everglades, and there
is hope of preserving all the known color forms of the Florida
tree snail.

Because of the great interest so many people have taken in
this snail, its life history has been well documented and recorded.

The arboreal *Liguus* comes down to the ground only during
its reproductive cycle: most of its probably four- or five-year
life span is spent in the trees where it finds its food, as well as
its resting place during the dry months.

The reproductive cycle of this hermaphrodite snail begins in
late summer, when two individuals get together and begin the
courtship that culminates in mating. Courtship consists of an
often lengthy ritual of caressing, in which the two partners
touch and rub against each other. Finally, one of them fertilizes
the other by inserting its copulatory organ into the genital pore
on the other's head. Shortly afterwards, the roles of male and

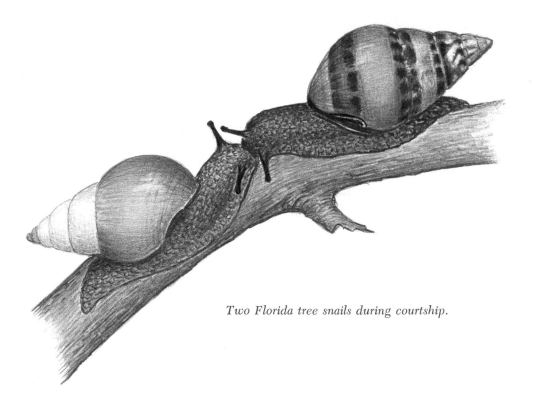

Two Florida tree snails during courtship.

female are switched as the second snail is also fertilized.

Several weeks later, both snails crawl down to the ground at the base of the tree. There each snail begins to dig the hole that will house its eggs. This is a long and laborious job for a creature whose foot is not a very efficient digging instrument, but within approximately twenty-four hours, the "nest," some three inches deep and shaped somewhat like a pear, is completed. Each snail deposits from two to four dozen eggs in the nest, covers it with leaf mold and soil, and then crawls back up its tree.

Now, while the eggs incubate in their snug underground nest, the adult snails begin to prepare for the resting period that will help them survive the long dry season ahead. After selecting a suitable branch, each snail withdraws into its shell, which it glues to the bark with a mucous secretion that, as it hardens, closes the aperture completely with a weathertight seal. This epiphragm remains in position until softened by the warm spring rains months later; at that time, the snail awakens, sticks its head out of the shell, and then begins to feed voraciously as it makes up for the long months of fasting.

In the meantime, the eggs have developed in their leaf-mold nests, and the same spring rains that awaken the dormant adult snails also bring forth the baby snails, which look like miniature adults. Although fully formed, their shells have only a few whorls and acquire two or three more in the first season, but only half again that much the next season, the growth slowing

Newly hatched Florida tree snails head for the nearest tree.

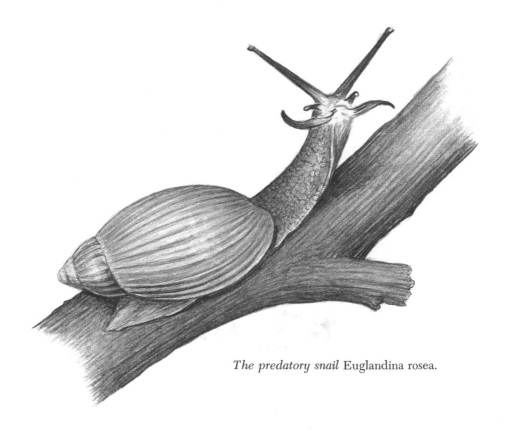

The predatory snail Euglandina rosea.

down progressively as they grow older. The age of a snail can thus be estimated by the number of whorls in its shell; an individual with eight whorls has to be at least two years old.

There are numerous natural enemies of the tree snail; they include not only birds, raccoons, opossums, and crabs, but also other snails. The light brown, streamlined predatory snail *Euglandina rosea* is one of the tree snail's most ferocious enemies. Moving much more swiftly than its victim, *Euglandina* attacks the helpless *Liguus* with a pair of dagger-shaped lips. Although the hapless tree snail tries to protect itself by withdrawing into its shell, that defense is of no avail because the predatory snail simply thrusts its head into the opening, and quite literally eats the legitimate owner out of its house.

The life histories of other tree snails are basically very similar to that of *Liguus,* differing only in details. Their appearance, however, may vary considerably. Many tree snails of tropical regions have elegantly shaped shells, beautiful bright colors, and handsome patterns, and some are coveted collectors' items. One such favorite is a pale green species delicately marked with white lines accentuating each individual whorl. Found only on a single island in New Guinea, this snail was first described in 1931.

Tree snails of the temperate zones are generally more uniform in shape and pattern, and also much less colorful, running mostly to browns, grays, and dull yellows. Very few of these

Shells of three exotic tree snails from Hawaii and the Philippines.

Three common European land snails. The one at top right is an arboreal species; the other two forage on the ground or in low plants.

arboreal snails are serious pests in their native habitats, where they are easily kept in check by their numerous natural enemies.

Among the abundant and economically important land snails of Europe are the members of the large genus *Helix*, and especially the species *Helix pomatica,* known locally as the vineyard snail. These edible snails are to be found on many menus in France, Italy, and other parts of central and southern Europe, where gourmets consider them a great delicacy.

Although the edible snails are sometimes collected after rains when they come out in great numbers, many are raised and fattened by suitable diets in special gardens. Four million edible snails were shipped to other parts of Europe from a region in southern Germany a century ago; today, most of the snails used for export to many countries come from France.

The genus *Helix* is represented in Europe by several species, but is also found in Asia and Africa. One of its most unusual members is the desert snail of Africa, *Helix desertorum,* which was discovered near an oasis in Egypt. In order to survive the extreme dry heat of such arid locations, the snail has to be able to close off the aperture of its shell with a lid so completely weathertight that no life-sustaining moisture can escape.

Helix pomatica, *the well-known edible snail of Europe.*

The species of the genus *Bulimus* are popularly known as "glutton snails," a designation that refers to their ravenous appetite for a variety of plants. Although most of them are tropical, and are found especially in the equatorial regions of South America, a few occur in Europe, including one in England that often makes its home in meadows grazed by sheep, which inadvertently eat the snails as they browse. According to an old popular belief, the meat of such sheep is supposed to be especially tasty, but scientists have found no evidence to support this assumption.

Another large genus of land snails is *Achatina,* which has some large and handsome members. The most famous—or infamous—is the African giant snail, mentioned earlier as an unwelcome immigrant to the United States. *Achatina fulica* is one of the most serious plant pests among snails. As its popular name indicates, it is a very large species, growing to the size of a lemon, and thus each individual consumes a lot of food; in addition, this species has the capacity to develop large populations—a single snail may lay batches of eggs, numbering from one hundred to four hundred, several times a year.

Originally limited to Africa, the giant snail has spread to Madagascar, India, the Philippines, Taiwan, and Hawaii. The infestation in Florida resulted from the release of three "pet" specimens that a child had brought home from Hawaii. It is now feared that, unless the snail can be eradicated in Florida, it may spread to Mexico and the west coast of the United States.

What makes this snail such a threat is its appetite for so many different plants economically important to man. Not only does it destroy leguminous crops, it also attacks citrus trees, causing the loss of large amounts of fruit. The worst damage to the citrus groves occurs when heavy infestations of giant snails kill young trees by eating the bark.

As though this were not enough, their appetite for calcium causes them to feed on paint containing this mineral, thus defacing the walls of houses and other structures, and this, together with their unsightly slime trails and excretions, constitutes a problem for any areas infested by large numbers of these snails. Efforts to control them center mainly on poisoned bait, since apparently no really effective natural enemies of this snail exist in the United States.

With the exception of just a single—and very small—representative in Europe, the members of *Achatina* occur only in warm regions and cannot survive in cold climates. Most of them are quite harmless to man's crops, and many are handsomely colored. *Achatina mauritiana* of Africa, for example, has a light yellowish shell patterned with fine multicolored lines.

Some very pretty, delicate, small species are found among the so-called glass snails and the amber snails, most of which are native to southern Europe and the Balkans. The shell of one familiar glass snail is thin and completely transparent, thus fully justifying its name. These snails can exist only in moist locations because they do not have the capability of preventing dehydration. In some species, the shell is not even large enough to permit the snail to withdraw completely into its house.

The snails whose shell is too small to accommodate the entire animal represent an intermediate development between the shell-bearing land species and the slugs that have no shell at all. Two large genera of such slugs, which include some economically important species, are *Limax* and *Arion*. Actually, many of them have a rudimentary shell, but it is usually buried in the mantle and not externally visible.

A number of slugs are serious agricultural pests; one of the most injurious is the small *Limax agrestis*, a voracious European species that destroys such crops as newly sprouted wheat and other grains. Because it may lay as many as one hundred eggs at a time, it can establish large populations if weather conditions are favorable. Its five-inch cousin *Limax maximus,* the spotted slug, may become a problem in cultivated gardens; other members of this group, however, are solitary, laying only a few eggs, and never occur in great numbers. Similarly, *Arion empiricorum,* a snail of deciduous woods, does very little harm. In any case, slugs in their natural environments are usually controlled by enemies such as toads. A few toads are also the best kind of "slug insurance" for private gardens, eliminating the need to use toxic chemicals.

The destructive European slug
Limax agrestis.

Typically slug-like in appearance despite the ridiculous little shell that sits, like a misplaced cap, on the back end of many of its species, are the slugs of the genus *Testacella,* which are distinguished from their relatives by certain anatomical features. Their feeding habits also vary considerably from those of other slugs, for they are carnivorous, displaying an appetite especially for earthworms. Being slow-moving, the slugs have to surprise the earthworms in order to capture them, for once the latter sense their enemy, they can disappear into the ground quickly enough to be safe from attack. The snails, however, possess a special weapon enabling them to capture an unsuspecting earthworm—a trunklike proboscis located between the lips, which the snail can thrust out suddenly to grab the worm before it can make good its escape.

A peculiar group of mostly tropical snails are the Auriculidae, represented especially by the species of the type genus *Auricula.* They often have very pretty elongated pointed shells with

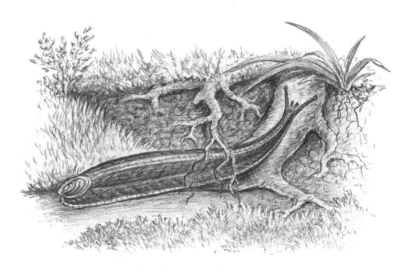

Predatory slug Testacella haliotidea, *known as the "greenhouse slug."*

A snail of the genus Auricula. *These snails are often found near brackish water.*

a strongly toothed aperture shaped like an ear. These pulmonate snails prefer brackish water, and are often found in salt marshes and along swampy seashores. Some of them seem to have taken up a primarily aquatic existence—a lifestyle that will be explored in the next chapter on the fully aquatic but air-breathing fresh-water snails.

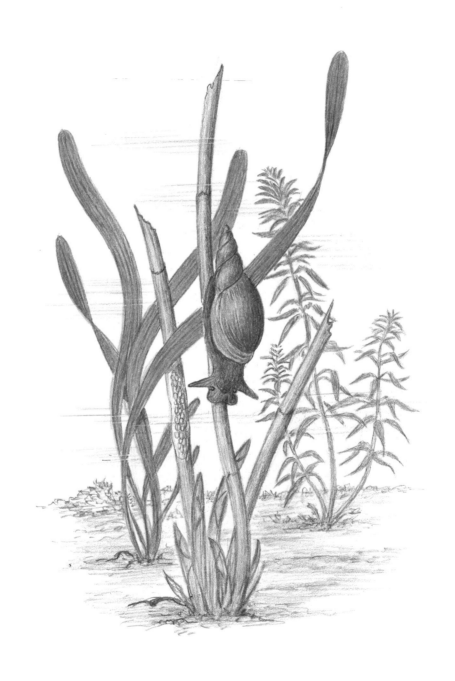

Fresh-Water Snails

It would be only logical to assume that snails living in rivers, streams, and ponds were originally marine species that adapted to life in fresh water. Although this is true of some, which have close relatives in the ocean as well as in brackish waters, the majority of fresh-water snails are really terrestrial types that returned to their original element. Their close relationship with the land snails is proved by the fact that they have lungs, instead of the gills that distinguish the marine species, and hence must periodically surface in order to breathe the air they need.

As noted in the preceding chapter, the group of land snails gathered in the family Auriculidae form a bridge between the purely terrestrial and the aquatic pulmonate snails, for some members are found near the shore in brackish water, and a number of South American species have invaded rivers and streams, where they are found in company with other fresh-water gastropods.

The pulmonate fresh-water snails are a large group of several families with a wide geographic distribution. While some are found mainly in warmer countries, a great many also occur in temperate zones. One widespread genus is *Lymnaea,* a group known as mud snails, many of which are common in stagnant waters of Europe, Africa, and the Americas. Among these snails are a number of species indirectly dangerous to man because they are the intermediary hosts for such parasites as the trematode worms *Bilharzia haematobia* and *Fasciata hepatica,* the liver fluke, which, as described earlier, attack both man and his domesticated animals. The cercaria—free-swimming tadpole-shaped larvae—of these worms can leave their snail hosts and survive for a relatively long period in the water, waiting for a warm-blooded host. Other fresh-water snails house flukes that, although not dangerous to man, may cause serious infestations in fish.

The common mud snail of Europe, *Lymnaea stagnalis,* is a typical representative of its group. A vegetarian like most fresh-water snails, it has a big appetite and eats large quantities of water plants. It is distinguished by a normally translucent, pointed shell that may attain a length of two and a half inches. Its wide head bears flat, triangular feelers that are not retractile; the eyes are located at the base rather than at the tip of the stalks. These snails can make themselves lighter or heavier by taking in or releasing varying amounts of air. If disturbed, the animal will simply release air from under its shell until it becomes heavier than water and sinks to the bottom. Normally, it can take in enough air to last it several hours. When its weight has been lightened by air bubbles, the mud snail can sometimes be seen "walking on the water" upside down, its foot gliding along the surface and its shell pointing downward.

Mud snails deposit their eggs in worm-shaped or oval

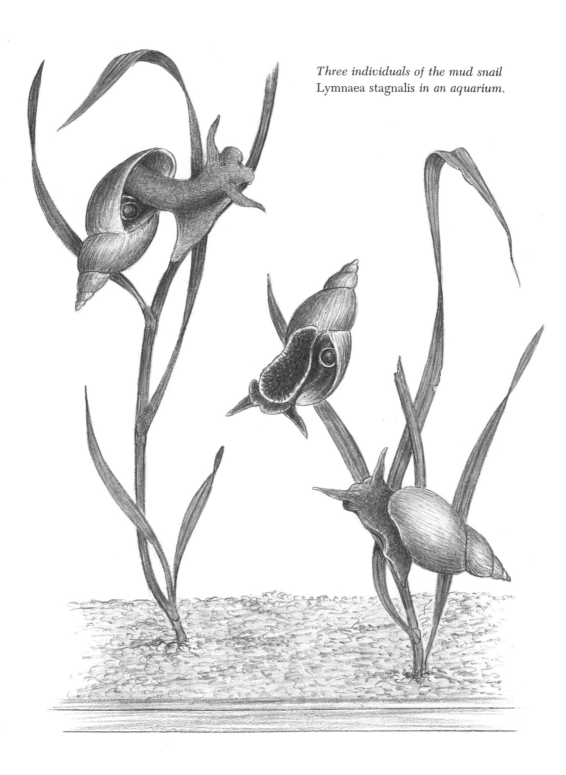

Three individuals of the mud snail Lymnaea stagnalis *in an aquarium.*

Shells of two common species
of the genus Lymnaea.

batches, usually on the undersides of water-plant foliage near
the surface. Each snail may produce up to twenty batches per
year, totaling from four hundred to two thousand eggs. Most of
them, of course, do not hatch as they fall prey to aquatic insects, fish, and other inhabitants of the ponds and pools.

Another large group of air-breathing fresh-water gastropods
is the genus *Planorbis,* the type genus of the family Planor-
biidae, known in Europe as plate snails because its members
are distinguished by a more or less flattened shell. Ramshorn
snails is another name for the members of this widely distributed group, which has many attractively colored species. Since
the ramshorn snails will consume quantities of uneaten food
in an aquarium, as well as some of the green algae slime that
accumulates on the glass, they are frequently kept in aquariums.
Some aquarium owners do not like to have any snails in their
tanks, claiming that they add to the pollution rather than help

Shell of a tropical ramshorn species.

eliminate it. In any event, keeping and observing fresh-water snails in a separate tank can be a most rewarding pastime.

The plate snails have eyes located at the base of their very slender feelers; in that feature, as well as in their ability to take in enough air in one "breath" to last them several hours, they resemble the mud snails. Their transparent eggs are deposited on smooth surfaces, such as the glass wall of an aquarium, so that the development of the young can be easily studied.

Curiously like the familiar marine limpets in appearance are the fresh-water snails of the genus *Ancylus,* often known as bowl snails because their shells look like inverted bowls. They

A common European ramshorn snail.

lead a more or less fixed existence, attaching themselves to water plants and moving about very little. The shells of these small snails are generally not very attractive.

The same certainly cannot be said of the members of the Ampullariidae, which are found in fresh-water bodies of warm regions. (Calling some of these stagnant pools "fresh water" is merely a euphemistic way of designating them as nonsaline.) Some of these snails are hefty individuals whose attractively colored and patterned shells may attain lengths of three inches or more. Known as apple shells to collectors, they are among the species also sold alive for use in aquariums; a large tropical kind called mystery snail is frequently imported by aquarium-supply wholesalers. These snails have both lungs and gills, and are therefore equipped for breathing either air or water—a very convenient and probably necessary arrangement, considering the oxygen-poor stagnant waters in which many of them live.

Moving from the pulmonate fresh-water species on to those that depend on some form of gills, we come to one of the most interesting of all these groups, the so-called swamp snails gathered in the family Vivipariidae. The name "swamp snail" is somewhat misleading because most of these gastropods do not live in swamps at all: their habitat includes ponds, pools, and moats, as well as rivers and streams, including some with relatively fast-flowing water.

Large tropical species of the genus Ampullaria.

The live-bearing swamp snail, Viviparus viviparus. *The animal has retired into the shell and closed off the aperture.*

Swamp snails consume all kinds of organic refuse including dead animals; in a pond, they fulfill—on a small scale, to be sure—a function similar to that of vultures and other terrestrial scavengers in the warm regions of the world.

The most fascinating fact about these snails, however, is that they—as their scientific family name implies—are live-bearing, which is an unusual mode of reproduction for gastropods. The type genus *Viviparus* is well represented in the temperate as well as in the warmer zones. In Europe, the large swamp snail *Viviparus viviparus,* whose greenish, brown-banded shell may attain a length of almost two inches, produces fully developed young throughout the summer months—but these young are born one at a time. The baby snails are about the size of a lentil at birth and have a shell consisting of several spirals.

The two smaller species of European live-bearing snails prefer very different habitats, for one is found in waters so stagnant and overgrown with algae that its shell, normally yellowish and translucent, is usually covered with a heavy coat of algae slime. The other seems to prefer rivers and streams whose water is not too fast-flowing.

Also equipped with gills are the mostly small and often pretty snails of the family Valvatidae, whose shells are shaped like spires. A peculiarity of this group—called comb snails in

A tropical fresh-water species of the genus Melania.

Europe—is the featherlike shape of their gills, attached only at the base so that their serrated tops protrude from the shell. The members of the type genus *Valvata* are found in North America and Europe, while those of the genus *Melania* occur in the warmer regions of the world. The attractive Malayan mud snail *Melania tuberculata*—which should not be confused with the mud snails of the genus *Lymnaea*—is frequently introduced into home aquariums because its habit of burrowing into the sand during the day loosens the soil and is therefore beneficial to the growth of water plants. These snails are active only at night, when they search for their food.

An interesting group of small fresh-water snails is found in the genus *Neritina*, which belongs to a family of mostly marine species. The several hundred members of the genus are found in many different parts of the world. Some of these snails, such as the black-and-white striped zebra shell, are quite handsome.

Shell of Neritina zebra, *a fresh-water snail with numerous marine relatives.*

The tiny European member of the group has a very thin but hard shell with a red or purplish criss-cross pattern. Observation of the development of these snails led to the discovery that, of the large number of eggs laid, only a few developed into young snails even when protected from predators. The puzzle was solved when close observation showed that the first of the hatchlings began to eat the other eggs until no more were left. This nutritious food makes the tiny cannibals grow very quickly, but at the expense of their less fortunate siblings: and so only a small percentage of each batch of eggs survives.

Although the land and fresh-water snails make up a group of several thousand species, we shall see in the following chapters that they cannot even begin to compete, in numbers as well as in variety, with the gastropods that inhabit the oceans of the world.

Snails of the Sea:
The Vegetarians

Because of the huge number of marine gastropods it is difficult to select, for a limited review such as this, individual species representative of all the important groups, and to present them in such a way that the text does not read like a checklist. Since this book stresses the living snails and their habits as much as the beauty of their shells, the sea snails have been grouped in two chapters according to their food preferences; one dealing with the vegetarians, and the second, with the carnivores—scavengers and predators alike—which include some of the most highly specialized and organized of all gastropods.

The abalones—members of the genus *Haliotis*—are well suited to begin the parade of vegetarian marine snails, for they are large, have beautiful shells, and tasty meat. Most of them occur in warmer waters. The California coast is the home of the largest of these species, the red abalone *Haliotis rufescens*, whose shell may measure a foot across. The black and green varieties are smaller, and the oriental and European abalones usually do not measure more than six inches.

The word "abalone" is of uncertain origin; in Germany, these snails are called sea ears because of their shape, and they are widely known elsewhere as ear shells. On the outside, abalone shells are usually rough and not very attractive; the insides display the familiar brilliant iridescence that has made Indian silver-and-abalone jewelry so justly popular. The iridescence in some abalones exhibits more of the blue-green band of the spectrum, and in others, the yellow-red band; the difference is caused by the spacing of the layers of thin platelets within the nacre.

The abalone's shell, which looks more like the half shell of a clam than a snail's shell, covers the animal like a roof as it clings to an underwater rock. The top has a small spiral, and the left side is punctured by a row of holes through which water reaches the gills and waste products are eliminated.

During the night, when they feed on seaweed, abalones move around quite a bit. However, they seem to stay largely within certain "home ground" areas, where they usually occur in numbers; during the day they remain hidden, attached to the undersides of rocks. The tenacity with which they cling to their sites, and the great strength they can exert with their large, muscular foot, was demonstrated by a near-tragic incident in California shortly after the turn of the century. A boy on an abalone hunt was almost drowned because he could not free his hand from beneath one of these large snails; his life was saved at the last moment by a young man who managed to break the powerful suction grip of the abalone.

One of the most familiar, as well as the least snail-like, groups of gastropods are the limpets. Actually, the shells popularly known as plate, cap, and keyhole limpets belong to different

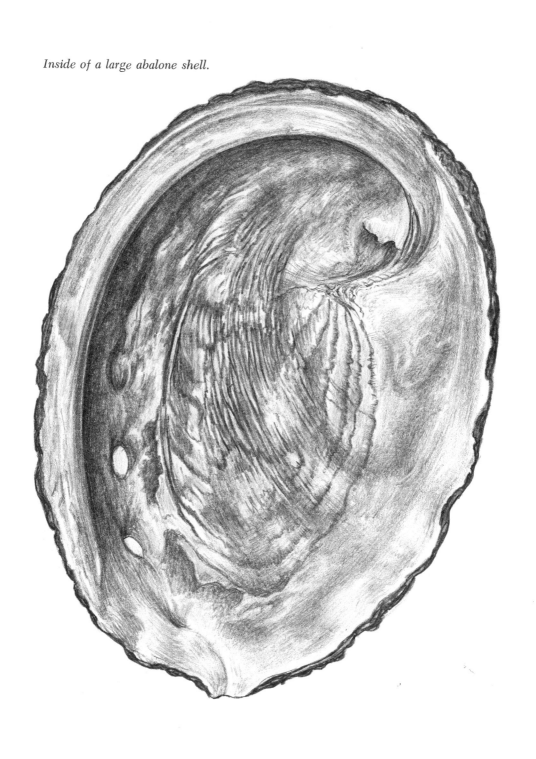

Inside of a large abalone shell.

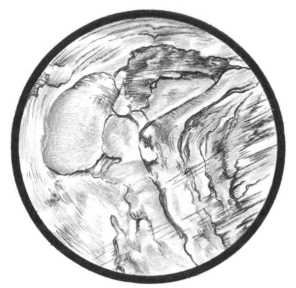

Enlarged portion of an abalone shell.

families, but in appearance as well as in habits, they are very similar. Although their free-swimming immature young display the typical spiral shell of the snail, that shell changes shape as the animal grows, turning into a flattened cone that all but hides the animal beneath. Limpets are usually found attached to rocks near the shore; once a mature animal has chosen a permanent site, it remains more or less stationary. Although the limpet shell displays a bilateral symmetry unusual for a snail, its coiled internal organs betray the derivation from typical spiral-shelled ancestors.

Abalone pearl, enlarged six times.

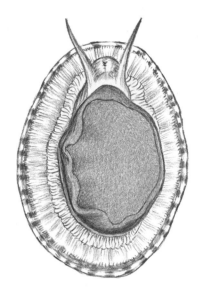

Live plate limpet from below.

Limpets, whose shells are generally drab-colored, with patterns of radiating stripes, are found predominantly in cooler waters; the familiar Atlantic plate limpet *Acmea testudinalis* and the common European *Patella vulgata* are typical examples of two of these groups. In the past, these small snails were important as food for the poorer inhabitants of Europe's coastal regions, and were collected in great numbers. Finding them is not difficult because they attach themselves to rocks and timbers between tide marks, and are exposed at low tide. Detaching them from their sites, however, is not always easy: a French scientist reported, as a result of his test of their adhesive power, that a weight of twenty-five pounds was needed to pull one of these snails off its site—a tenacity reflected in the use of the word "limpet" for a person difficult to dislodge from the office or position he holds.

Limpets graze on seaweed, moving slowly over the rocks while they eat: because of a well-developed homing instinct,

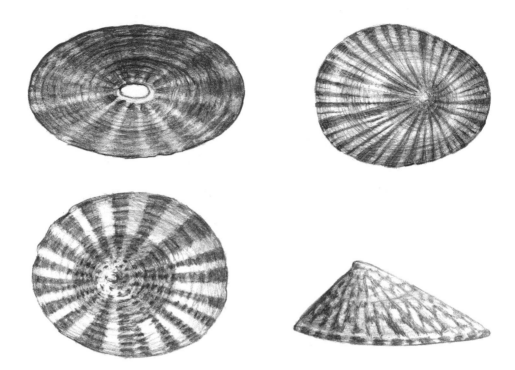

Four different species of limpets. From left to right: (top) Darwin's keyhole limpet; black-lined limpet. Bottom: greenish cap limpet; Atlantic plate limpet.

they can find the way back to their original site with a remarkable degree of accuracy.

Keyhole limpets, whose shells look like tiny volcanoes, belong to yet another family but resemble the true limpets in appearance as well as in lifestyle; the chief outward difference is the hole at the peak of the shell that has given them their popular name.

Much sought after by collectors are members of two closely related families, the Trochidae and Turbinidae, known as top and turban shells, respectively. Great confusion exists in the use of these popular names, exemplified by such species as the wavy top shell of California, which is really a member of the turban shell group. Only the use of scientific names can insure correct identification.

The common names of both groups were inspired by the shape of the shell displayed by most members; that of the Trochidae looks like a children's top, whereas that of the Turbinidae resembles an oriental turban. More than a dozen species of turbans and several times that number of top shells are found in North American waters; the chestnut turban and the channeled top of Florida waters are representative examples.

Many of the exotic species are large and have beautiful iridescent shells. Thus the interior of the five-inch pyramid top shell of the Indo-Pacific region was long used for the manufacture of such mother-of-pearl articles as buttons and jewelry. Similarly, the shell of the pitcher snail *Turbo olearis,* found on the rocky coasts of the Spice Islands near New Guinea, provided much of the exceptionally fine mother-of-pearl used by the Chinese for the exquisite inlay work which adorns their intricately fashioned boxes, cupboards, and other furniture.

Both the top and turban snails feed on a variety of marine algae, of which there is an abundant supply in the shallow or moderately deep waters they prefer. Although these snails are not eaten in America, some of the larger kinds especially are important food items in Asia.

Special physical characteristics shared by many species of both the top and turban shells are fringes and filaments adorning various parts of the body, and a snout-like elongation of the head. The operculum of the top shells is usually rather thin; that of the turbans, however, is thick and hard, permitting them to close off the opening of the shell very efficiently—a fact

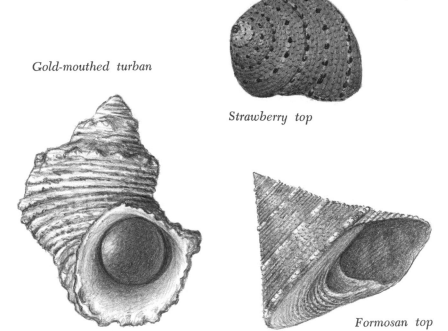

Gold-mouthed turban

Strawberry top

Formosan top

Three members of the top and turban families. The aperture of the turban shell at left is closed by the globular operculum.

that contributes to the ability of some species to survive prolonged periods out of water and in dry surroundings. Thus individuals of the species known as the East Indian pagoda snail, which frequents rocks just above water level but moistened by the spray of breakers that roll in against the cliffs, reportedly lived for several months without either water or food.

An unusual and interesting feature found in the pheasant shells, a small family with beautifully variegated patterns closely related to the two preceeding groups, is the detachable portion of the foot. This very handy protective device often permits such a snail seized by an enemy to save its life while leaving the detachable foot portion with the predator as a consolation prize. The snail's foot later regenerates itself, which is a feature characteristic of a number of invertebrates, but is also found is some lizards, which can break off a portion of the tail that is later replaced by new growth.

The Neritidae are a family that includes marine members as well as the fresh-water species discussed in the preceding chapter. The marine species are found mainly in warm waters near the shore, and even in estuaries, where they attach themselves to rocks and pilings, usually above the high-water line. Most are small; a two-inch species is considered quite large.

Among the best known of all univalve mollusks are the periwinkles, a group of generally small snails many of which measure less than an inch long. The common periwinkle *Littorina*

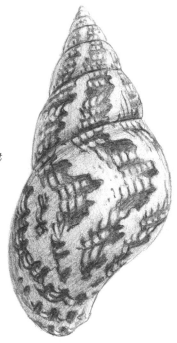

One variant of the Australian pheasant shell Phasianella.

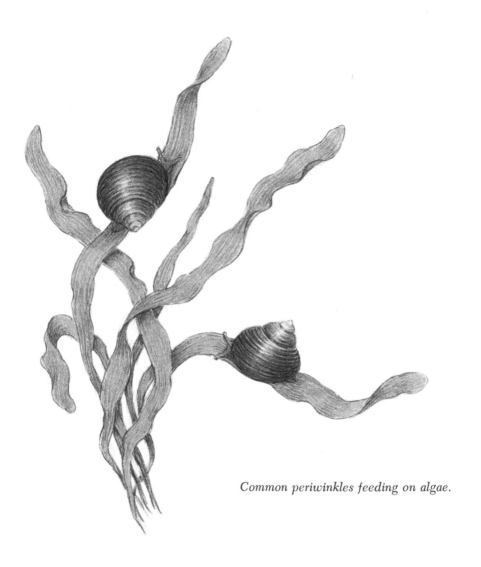

Common periwinkles feeding on algae.

littorea of the Atlantic coast was very probably introduced from Europe, and quickly established itself in its American habitat. Unlike some other unwelcome gastropod "immigrants," this harmless vegetarian has caused no problems, but it has failed to become a favorite sea food among Americans, as it is for many Europeans.

Periwinkles are always found near the shore on algae and submerged rocks and timber; many are also capable of tolerating varying degrees of salinity. In addition, they are noted for their ability to survive out of water for prolonged periods.

The shells of the periwinkles are generally drab, brownish or grayish; the famous periwinkle blue refers to the color of a flower. Although the snail and the plant share the same name, the origin of each appears to be quite different.

Three closely related groups with typically long, thin, pointed shells are the turret, telescope, and horn snails. Other close relatives, such as the attractive sundials with their widely coiled, flattened spirals have very similar habits despite their different appearance.

All these snails prefer shallow water; many are found in tidal pools in the mud and on the seaweed. They feed on a variety of marine plants, with eelgrass being a favorite of many species.

Horn snails are by far the largest of these groups; for the most part they occur in tropical and subtropical waters. Turret snails are found in temperate as well as in tropical zones; the telescope snails, on the other hand, are an exclusively tropical family. Known as "creepers" because they are commonly found crawling around in the mud flats of estuaries, they often have attractively shaped, pagoda-like shells; unfortunately, the acid content of the brackish water in which they live tends to erode the shell. Fine examples of turret and telescope shells are the great screw shell of *Turritella terebra* of the Indian Ocean, and that of the Queensland creeper of Australian waters; both snails attain a length of five inches, and have beautifully sculptured shells.

Distinguished by a relatively fixed existence similar to that of the limpets are the slipper snails, also variously called boat shells and cup-and-saucer shells. All these names refer to the

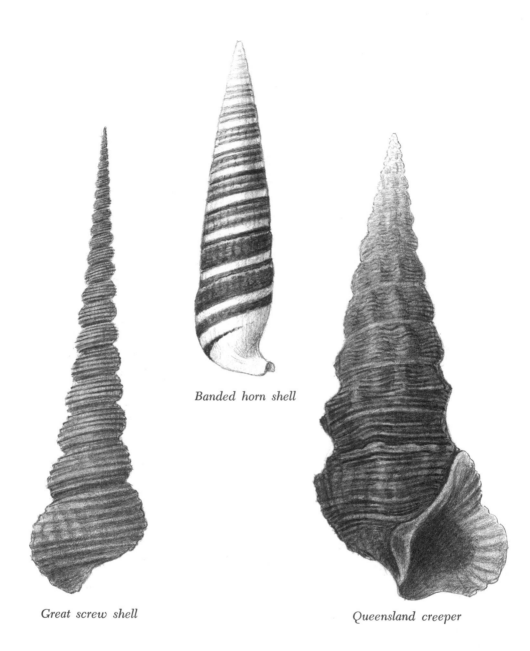

Banded horn shell

Great screw shell

Queensland creeper

Representatives of the turret, telescope, and horn shells, three closely related groups.

plate inside the shell that has made observers compare it variously to a slipper, a boat, or a cup on a plate, although the resemblance is far-fetched in all instances.

Slipper snails live in shallow water in all temperate and tropical seas. One of the largest and most attractive of the North American species is the onyx slipper, which is a deep chocolate brown with a white "boat deck" inside the shell. These snails are usually found attached to stones or to other, larger shells, and move from their home sites only to feed. They are interesting not so much for their shells, which usually do not have striking colors or patterns, but for their habit—most unusual among gastropods—of brooding their eggs. The female slipper snail has been observed gathering the egg mass under its foot, so that the shell covers and protects the brood along with the mother.

Among the best known of all marine gastropods are the conchs and their kin; not all shells called conchs, however, belong in this group, which includes the peculiar scorpion and tibia shells. Conchs are found in all the warmer seas with the

An onyx slipper shell seen from below.

Spindle tibia

Arthritic spider conch

Dove conch

exception of the Mediterranean; many live in deep water. Some members of the group are distinguished by extreme modifications of the shell, with numerous leg-like projections, especially of the lip, which explains names such as "tibia" and "spider."

The shell of the queen conch *Strombus gigas* of the West Indies may attain a length of a foot, and a weight of several pounds; with its glazed rose-pink aperture, it is one of the most striking of all shells. The meat of this snail is edible and of importance as a staple seafood in the Caribbean, where conch

The famous queen, or pink, conch shell.

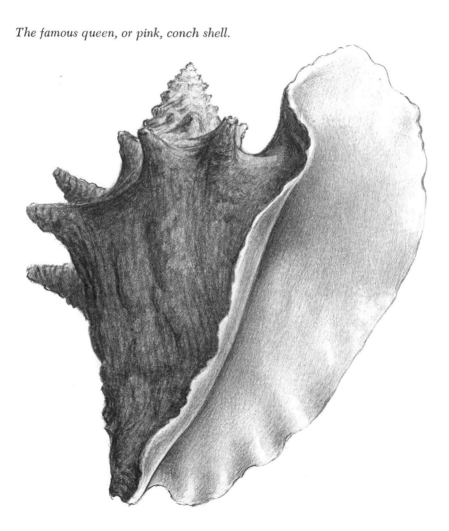

fishing provides a livelihood for many. Legislation now regulates the take of conchs along the coasts of Florida to a certain extent to help prevent abuse.

The horny, sickle-shaped operculum is a peculiar feature of many members of the group typified by the genus *Strombus* and known as Strombidae. By digging this claw-like "foot" into the sand, the animals can propel themselves forward in a series of short hops when fleeing from enemies, or during the search for food. Although conch snails are primarily vegetarian, some seem to feed on dead animal matter at least occasionally.

A truly unique habit distinguishes the small group of snails known as Xenophoridae—from the Greek words *xenos,* foreign, and *phoros,* bearing—which are popularly known as carrier shells. Both the scientific and the common names refer to their strange predilection of picking up, and glueing to their shell, small foreign objects such as other shells, pebbles, and bits of coral. Some of these snails are such avid "shell collectors" that their own shell may disappear completely beneath the assortment of smaller shells and other objects cemented all over the outer surface.

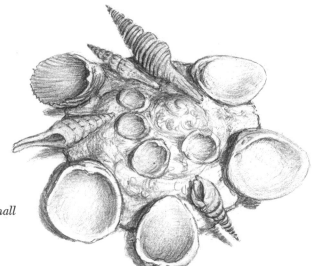

*Pallid carrier snail with small
shells attached to its own.*

Carrier snails live in both shallow and deep waters; although the species found at greater depths are usually less efficient collectors, they frequently have, attached to their own shell, some rare or unusual shell coveted by human collectors. There seems to be little doubt that, whatever the reason for this peculiar habit, it acts as a protective device that helps to camouflage the carrier snail's own shell, and also makes attacks by some enemies more difficult. Such conjectures do not, however, offer any explanation of the phenomenon, nor do they make it any less fascinating; it remains one of the numerous intriguing mysteries encountered by any student of animal behavior in the course of his observations.

Although the carrier snails appear to be largely vegetarian, it is believed that they occasionally are scavengers, feeding on any type of organic matter including dead sea animals; they thus form a link to the carnivorous species discussed in the following chapter.

Snails of the Sea: The Carnivores

Marine snails preferring meat, rather than a plant diet, include the scavengers, which feed on dead animals, and the predators, which attack and eat living prey consisting of other mollusks, echinoderms, polyps, and even fish. The carnivorous species include the most highly evolved of all gastropods.

Among the oddest-looking of the more primitive species are the worm snails, whose popular name refers to the corkscrew-shaped shells. Their life history is most unusual, even though it begins normally enough when the female lays her eggs, which are enclosed, in numbers ranging from ten to thirty, in tiny transparent bags. The embryos hatching from those bags are no larger than a pinhead, but are equipped not only with the velum, which is the swimming organ of the gastropod larvae, but also with a delicate transparent shell.

Up to that point and throughout the larval stage, the development of the young worm snail is quite typical of that found

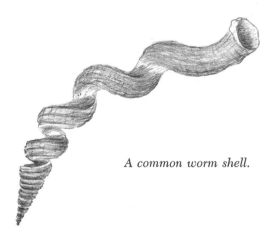

A common worm shell.

in other marine gastropods; soon, however, all is changed as the young snail attaches its shell to coral or a stone, or embeds it in a sponge. From that point on, the shell, which until then was a steep spire, begins to grow in the loose, white or brownish corkscrew-like coils that distinguish the species of this group. The shells are very hard; collectors walking around barefoot frequently gash their feet badly on the razor-sharp edges of the apertures.

Color Code

Body: tan
Eggs: blue
Foot: orange
Head: pink
Mantle: yellow
Operculum: green
Shell: brown

Diagram of a worm snail with eggs;
part of the shell is removed.

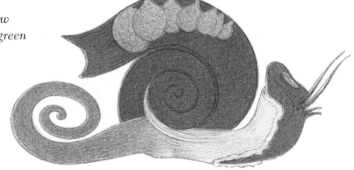

Shell of the precious wentletrap.

Since worm snails cannot move around, they have to wait for their food to come close enough to be seized and eaten; although no exact information about the diet of worm snails exists, it appears they feed mainly on plankton, minute marine creatures that they collect in long mucous strings. Tests with captives proved them to be not particularly shy, and willing to accept bits of proffered food.

An interesting group of marine snails that lives on invertebrates with poisonous stings includes the wentletraps and the violet snails. Wentletraps are found in temperate and tropical waters, and are greatly prized for their delicately shaped and sculptured shells, which in most cases have a glazed white or ivory surface. The word is of Dutch derivation, from *wentle*, winding, and *trap* (*Treppe* in German), staircase. *Epitonium pretiosa*, the precious wentletrap, used to be one of the most coveted of these shells; the largest in a family of rather small species is the rare Japanese magnificent wentletrap *Amaea magnifica*, whose shell many attain a length of five inches.

Shell of a violet snail of the genus Janthina.

Most wentletraps live in fairly deep water, where they feed on a variety of invertebrates and especially on sea anemones, whose powerful poison stings do not seem to bother them. It is believed that the violet dye exuded by the wentletraps may act as an anesthetic that paralyzes their prey before they attack it.

Even more interesting are the habits of a related group, the violet snails of the family Janthinidae. Pelagic species that live in the open sea of warmer regions, they are frequently washed ashore by storms and die because they cannot crawl back into the water. Empty shells may drift over great distances and wind up on the beaches of cooler latitudes. The first thing that strikes the observer as very special about these delicate, fragile shells is their beautiful violet-blue coloring, one of the rarest of all hues found in shells.

Even more unusual than their appearance, the lifestyle of the janthids has fascinated naturalists for centuries. They have no eyes, and accordingly cannot see their prey, which consists largely of jellyfish; instead, they seem to recognize these coelenterates by touch when they encounter them while floating along in the open sea. In order to float, the violet snail constructs a raft made of air-filled mucous bubbles, to which it clings upside down with its foot. Sometimes large numbers of these snails join their rafts together to form huge floats; one such float off the coast of Florida was reported to be ninety miles long!

Live violet snail Janthina fragilis, *with attached bubble float as seen from above.*

An interesting symbiotic relationship seems to exist between the violet snails and a small bluish-purple crab that inhabits the bubble rafts. The crab gets transportation and probably food from this association; to what extent the snails benefit has not yet been established.

When a violet snail encounters a hydroid such as a Portuguese man-of-war, it leaves its float and crawls on the underside of its prey. Like the wentletraps, there it exudes a dye of a deep purplish color, which is believed to anesthetize the stinging cells of the jellyfish.

Unlike most other marine gastropods, violet snails are hermaphrodites, with each individual capable of developing both male and female reproductive organs. Self-fertilization of the snail's eggs is prevented by the time lapse in the development of the sex organ. Thus a snail in the male phase fertilizes another individual in the female phase. Later, roles are reversed as the first snail, now a female, is fertilized by a partner in the male phase.

Some violet snails deposit their eggs on the underside of their floats; others, such as the common *Janthina janthina,* are viviparous, giving birth to larval young.

Of all the shells, none have been more highly prized by peoples of different cultures than the smooth, glazed, al-

The handsome mole cowrie of the Indo-Pacific.

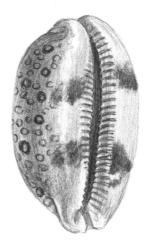

Shell of the eyed cowrie from above and below.

most egg-shaped shells of the famous cowries. The early naturalists who named this group expressed their admiration for the beautiful cowries in the family name Cypraeidae, which is derived from Cypria, or Venus, the goddess of love. In older books, cowries are often called Venus shells.

The most distinctive feature of the cowrie shell is its lack of an externally visible spiral structure. Only young cowries still have that typical structure; later on in the life of the animal, lime deposits progressively cover and obliterate the individual whorls. At the same time, the pigments that create specific colors and patterns are deposited, so that—to a certain degree —it is possible to tell the age of a cowrie from the coloring and shape of its shell. Those of young snails are usually grayish and drab; a fully mature adult, on the other hand, has the highly glazed and often handsomely colored shell prized by collectors. That shell will then no longer grow or change in hue, regardless of how much longer the animal lives.

Cowries are inhabitants of warmer waters; the North American species are limited to the coastal regions of the southern states. On the Pacific coast, only a single species of the type genus *Cypraea* is found.

One of the most popular cowries—reputed in the past to have been reserved only for Fiji chieftains—is the golden cowrie *Cypraea aurantium*. Other favorites are the eyed cowrie and the map cowrie, both from the Indo-Pacific. A handsome North American species is the chestnut cowrie with its rich brown tones.

The mantle of the living cowrie is often so large that it all but envelops the shell, and thus contributes to the preservation of the highly glazed, smooth surface. The head of the cowrie is usually fairly chunky, its feelers thin and closely set. Like

Live chestnut cowrie. The mantle envelopes much of the shell.

Shell of the southern moon snail.

many other snails, cowries have a siphon, or spout, formed by a portion of the mantle, that aids in respiration. They feed on coral and other small invertebrates.

Interesting especially for their breeding habits are a certain sand-dwelling species known popularly as moon snails because of their typically rounded, almost globular shells. The size of its unusually large foot can be increased by absorption of water; the moon snail uses this foot to engulf a clam or other bivalve, whose flesh it devours after drilling a neat circular hole through the shell with its file-like radula. Some species are scavengers, eating dead fish and other sea animals.

When the time for egg-laying arrives, female moon snails produce a sticky mucous secretion, which, mixed with sand grains, they use to cement the eggs into collar-shaped flexible rings about the thickness of an orange peel. Held against the light, these collars appear to be dotted with small semitransparent cells containing a yellow center; those are the eggs. The sand-and-mucus mass in which the eggs are embedded affords

Egg ring of a moon snail.

them considerable protection. For a long time, early naturalists believed these "sand collars" to be colonies of tiny polyps.

Noteworthy for a variety of reasons are the tritons and their kin, the helmet, tun, and fig snails. Tritons were mentioned more than two thousand years ago in the poems of ancient Rome; the original Roman war trumpet, the *buccina*, is believed to have been a large triton shell. Halfway around the world in the Far East, one of the largest of all gastropods, which also served as a war trumpet, is the huge triton *Cymatium variegatum*, whose shell may attain a length of twenty inches.

Shells of the helmet snails, closely allied to the tritons, have been used as ornaments for centuries. They have very thick, heavy shells with varicolored layers; today they are used for cameos and other kinds of jewelry.

Like the tritons, helmet snails are found in warmer regions; they prefer shallow water, where they hunt echinoderms such as starfish, their favorite food. A distinctive feature of the living animal is the veil-like portion of the mantle over the head, which forms a long siphon; another is the modification of the mouthparts into a proboscis. Large and handsome North American species are the emperor and king helmets of the southern coasts, both of which may attain a length of nine inches, and the horned helmet of the Indo-Pacific, which my be a foot long.

Distinguished by thin shells that appear too small for the animal are the tun and fig snails; as they crawl around, the oversized foot protrudes on all sides beyond the rim of the shell, and in the fig snails, the head with its short triangular feelers is completely hidden when seen from above. These snails prefer the sandy bottom of the sea, where they hunt for their prey; the common fig snail of the southern Atlantic Coast is between three and four inches long.

Tun snails have interesting feeding habits; in the manner of the moon snails they engulf their prey with their oversized foot, and then partially digest it in the oral cavity with the help of their acid saliva. This saliva, which is secreted by a large

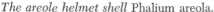

The areole helmet shell Phalium areola.

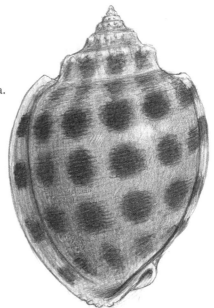

*Representatives of the triton, tun,
and fig shell groups.*

Giant tun

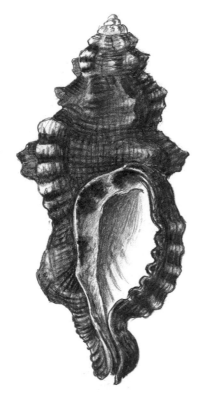

Washer triton

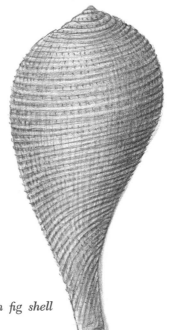

Common fig shell

gland, serves also as a defensive weapon, for tun snails have been observed spraying it at intruders with their trunk-like proboscis.

One of the largest and most widely distributed of all marine snail groups is the genus *Murex* and its close relatives, which number about a thousand species, and are found in all temperate and warm waters. Many strange and bizarre shell forms distinguish the snails of this group, which include the oyster drills, purples, and dogwinkles. Well-known North American species are the apple murex, the lace murex, and the Atlantic oyster drill of ill repute. As the name implies, these snails are capable of drilling holes through the shells of oysters and other bivalves with their file-like tongue and then eating the animal out of its shell.

As mentioned in the first chapter, members of *Murex* were the "purple-dye" snails of ancient times. The yellowish gland that contains the dye can be seen when the mantle of the snail is opened; under the influence of sunlight, the light yellow liquid secreted by this gland turns into an indelible purplish violet.

Color Code

Body: red
Gills: blue
Head: yellow
Mantle: green
"Purple" gland: purple

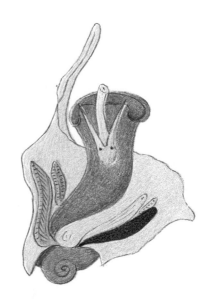

Diagram of a murex snail with the "purple gland" exposed.

Today, although the dye is no longer of any importance, the oddly shaped and often spectacular shells are in great demand by collectors; one of the most bizarre is the Venus comb of the Western Pacific. The largest species is the branched murex of the Indo-Pacific region; its shell may be a foot long.

Small relatives of the murex snails, the coral snails, have elegantly sculptured shells. Most of them have lost their radula, and have become parasitic feeders on coral, in which some species completely embed themselves. The majority occur in the Indo-Pacific region.

Among the best-known marine snails are the whelks and their kin. They are a huge group numbering several thousand spe-

Live dye snail Murex brandaris.

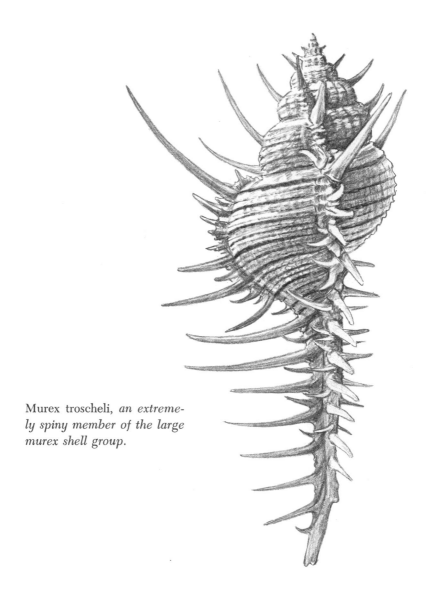

Murex troscheli, *an extremely spiny member of the large murex shell group.*

cies, and include the two largest gastropods in the world. Whelks and their relatives are found in all temperate and warm waters; some occur even in polar seas where relatively few other snails are found.

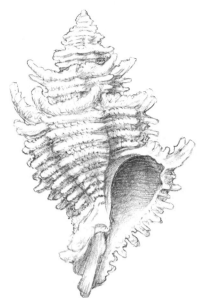

Latiaxis kirana, *a delicately sculptured white coral snail relative.*

A familiar North American species is the lightning, or left-handed, whelk of the Gulf coast. Its shell is one of the few with a counter-clockwise spiral. The animal also is unusual in that it is jet black, in sharp contrast to the light coloring of the shell. The largest of all the whelks is the Australian band snail, which attains a length of two feet.

Many whelks are predatory, drilling through the shells of bivalves to feed on the animals inside; others are primarily scavengers. Some species are widely used by man as food, especially in Europe but also along the North American Atlantic coast.

Whelks deposit their eggs in horny cases often strung together in long rows and attached to various objects. Each case contains a large number of eggs, yet not all the young eventually emerge, because the early hatchlings feed on the other eggs, a phenomenon already noted in the snails of the genus *Neritina.*

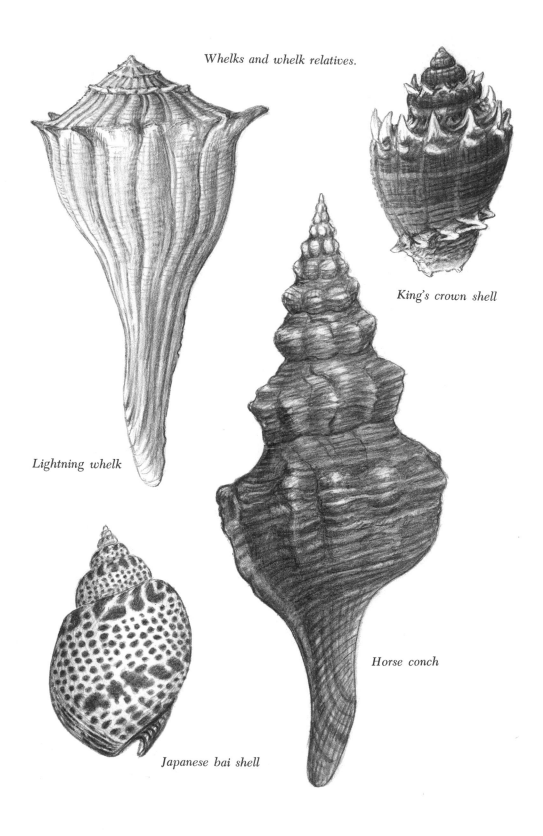

Whelks and whelk relatives.

King's crown shell

Lightning whelk

Horse conch

Japanese bai shell

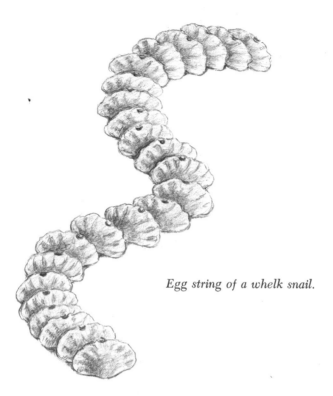

Egg string of a whelk snail.

Hefty, large whelk relatives are the tulip snails; the Florida horse conch, which despite its name belongs in the whelk group, may occasionally reach a length of two feet, as large as the giant Australian band snail. Both the animal and its shell are handsomely colored and make star attractions in marine aquariums.

A great variety of shell forms and patterns is displayed by the volutes and their kin, which include the olives, miters, and harps. Many olive shells resemble cowries; most miters have steeply spiralled, pointed shells; and the harp shells have raised ribs that give them the fancied resemblance to the musical instrument.

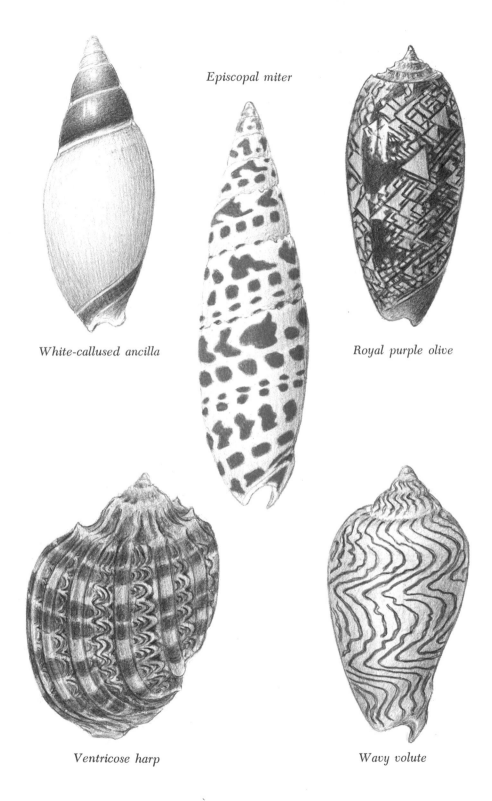

Episcopal miter

White-callused ancilla

Royal purple olive

Ventricose harp

Wavy volute

Most of these snails live in warmer waters; a few olives extend into northern latitudes. The North American species, such as the lettered olive, are light-colored; those from subtropical and tropical regions often have rich, deep hues.

Olive snails are fairly fast crawlers; they feed on dead marine animals. The foot of the olives is broad and usually folded over the shell on the sides; the mantle is enlarged into a siphon.

Distinguished also by a broad foot, the volutes have habits similar to those of the olives. Most are found in the tropics and are brightly colored. A handsome species is Juno's volute of the southern United States; another favorite of collectors is the music volute, *Voluta musica,* of the Caribbean, whose dark markings resemble a musical score.

The most highly evolved of the marine snails are the cones and their allies, the turrid and auger snails. Turrids are found in tropical waters usually at considerable depths. The shapes of the shells differ greatly in the various species; many are long, slender, and pointed; others may be short and globular; some resemble a large screw.

Perhaps the most intriguing shell-bearing marine gastropods are the cones, the large majority of which occur in the Indo-Pacific region, although some fifty species are found in American waters. Familiar species from the Florida coast are the crown, alphabet, and Florida cones. The shells of these snails display a profusion of beautiful patterns and colors that have made them a collector's delight. Naturalists have been at least equally fascinated by the venom apparatus with which these snails are equipped, and which has resulted in their being called the rattlesnakes among mollusks.

The fact that these snails have a venomous bite has been known for centuries. The Dutch naturalist, G.E. Rumphius, reported in 1705 that a woman in Indonesia died after having

Marbled cone

General cone

Babylon turrid

Episcopal cone

Maldive cone

picked up a live cone while fishing. All she felt was a faint sting-ing sensation in her hand, but soon after, she became uncon-scious, and a short while later she was dead. Several other hu-man fatalities have been reported; not all cone snails can deliver a fatal bite, but the large ones especially should be handled with caution.

Although cones are often said to have a poisonous sting, they actually bite. They inject the poison through tiny hollow teeth less than a tenth of an inch long. The potency of the venom is indicated by the minute quantities these teeth can inject. Cone venom varies with the species; some are effective only against certain types of prey, such as other snails, fish, or worms.

Cone snails hunt at night. Sensing the presence of prey—probably through a chemical sensor ejected into the water—the cone extends its proboscis and bites its victim. Actually, the snail's teeth remain in the victim's body, and pass through the snail's digestive system along with its food. New teeth are formed to replace the ones that have been used by the predator.

Fish-eating cones often bury themselves in the sand with only the siphon protruding. When a fish approaches, the snail bites it, injecting a dart, and then expands its oral cavity to engulf the paralyzed victim.

Because fish are vertebrates, the venom effective against them is also most dangerous to humans. Human fatalities seem to have been caused exclusively by fish-eating cones, of which the textile cone appears to be the deadliest.

The auger snails, relatives of the cones, with long tapered, often very colorful shells, have poison glands similar to those of the cones, and use them to paralyze the marine worms on which they feed. They are an exclusively tropical group found in the Indo-Pacific region.

With these highly evolved snails completing our review of the important groups of shell-bearing species, we shall meet in the following chapter the strange, predominantly shell-less species that have to be seen alive to appreciate their often striking beauty of form and color.

Shell of the dimidiate auger.

Sea Slugs, Sea Hares, and Bubbles

If the title of this chapter sounds like an odd assortment, it sounds exactly right: it would be difficult to assemble a more peculiar group of animals than these gastropods. Because most have no shell, they are of little interest to the shell collector and are therefore generally not well known; yet many are beautifully colored and patterned, and have complex and fascinating lifestyles.

The bubble snails, although closely related to completely shell-less kinds, are often much more handsomely colored than their thin, fragile shells, which usually are too small to allow the animal to withdraw completely into it. Most species prefer warm, shallow waters, but a number also live in temperate regions. North American species include the California bubble and the eastern paper bubble. A European species, *Aceras bullata,* is common along the coasts of the North Sea and the Mediterranean.

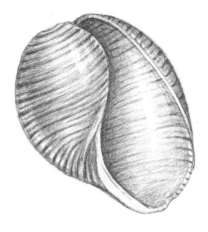

The brown-lined paper bubble, one of the more common bubble shells.

The fully extended foot of such a snail is a most peculiar sight. It is so broad that it can be folded over the shell from both sides so that only a small triangular portion of the shell is visible. When disturbed, the snail withdraws its body into the folds of the foot, and then looks like a soft, slimy globe, or bubble.

The versatility of the foot is not exhausted by its function as both a vehicle for crawling and a protective wrap for the snail; it is also a swimming organ, and it serves to propel the animal through the water for a few minutes at a time. Observers describe the swimming of the bubble snail as a seemingly effortless rhythmic movement that looks as though the animal is flying under water.

Most bubble snails are predators; some, however, seem to be omnivorous scavengers that feed on all kinds of organic material. The related canoe shells are predators that hunt out and eat other gastropods.

Still equipped with shells, even though they are very small and thin, are some species of a group whose scientific and common names both refer to their mode of locomotion. The Pteropoda, meaning the wing-footed ones, are most peculiar-looking creatures, so far removed from what a snail is supposed to look like that few people would recognize them as members of the group. Their common name, sea butterflies, is a descriptive term, for they propel themselves through the water with a fluttering motion of the winglike lobes of the mantle. Pteropods occur in all temperate and warm waters; they are found in the open sea near the surface, where they feed on tiny crustaceans and other plankton; they themselves, in turn, furnish an important part of the food for certain whales and large fishes.

The strange-looking sea slugs and their relatives have intrigued people for ages, a fact that resulted in some queer stories and superstitions attaching to some of these gastropods. Prominent among them is the sea hare, a name given to certain close relatives of the bubble snails. Although the sea hares appear to be entirely without a shell, actually they do have a small horny or calcified shield-like shell buried in the mantle.

From the appearance of this snail with its double pair of tentacles, the longer of which bears a striking resemblance to the long ears of a hare, it is not difficult to see how it came by

Two different species of pteropods, small, largely colorless snails of the high seas.

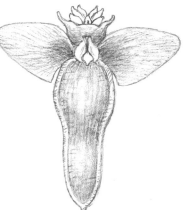

its popular name. In addition, sea hares move slowly about the bottom, feeding on whatever seaweed they can find, thereby strengthening the resemblance to a grazing mammal, which perhaps explains why a common English species is popularly known as the "sea cow."

Over the centuries, fishermen have told some hair-raising—or rather hair-removing—stories about the sea hares, including the fantastic claims that their secretions will make the hair fall out, and that their pungent odor causes strong men to faint. The old scientific name of one common species of sea hares was *Aplysia depilans*—literally, the "hair-removing unwashed one"—hardly a very complimentary term, and proof of the influence that popular tales had on the naturalists who originally named the animal.

A sea hare emitting a purplish, ink-like substance, a typical defense of many mollusks.

Stripped of these exaggerations, the facts about the secretion of those sea hares found in temperate waters are much less sensational, for it is a dark, purplish fluid similar to that produced by many marine snails, as well as other mollusks such as cuttlefish and octopuses, all of which emit dark-colored secretions when frightened. That of the sea hares is mildly irritating only to hypersensitive persons; some tropical species, however, do have secretions capable of causing a burning sensation on the skin. None of them can make hair fall out, although that story made an interesting sailors' yarn.

The common sea hare of Europe is about six inches long, but some of its tropical relatives attain almost twice that length. Normally, the winglike lobes of the foot with which the animal can swim are held upright and undulate slightly as it crawls slowly along the bottom. However, the lobes can be folded over the back in a way that completely hides the small shell and the tube that forms the entrance to the gills.

Closely related to the sea hares are certain species whose gills are not covered by a calcified shield, but are, instead, located under the edge of the mantle. The body of such a snail looks like an egg-shaped dome when seen from above; a small head with short tentacles is visible at one end. Some species have a small, thin shell that covers only a portion of the animal. These snails normally do not move around much, preferring to hide under large stones. When disturbed, their defense consists in curling up like an armadillo and letting themselves sink to the bottom, where they remain until they believe the intruder to be gone.

The preceding groups mentioned in this chapter all have some sort of covering for their respiratory organs; those that follow have none at all, explaining why they are called nudibranchs, which means naked, or uncovered, gills. Popularly, these snails, most of which are found in temperate waters, are known as sea slugs, for many resemble terrestrial slugs in general body shape, and none of the adults possess even the vestige of a shell still present in the sea hares and their relatives. The larval forms of the nudibranchs have delicate little shells that

A nudibranch typified by bush- or leaf-like gills arranged in a circle on the back.

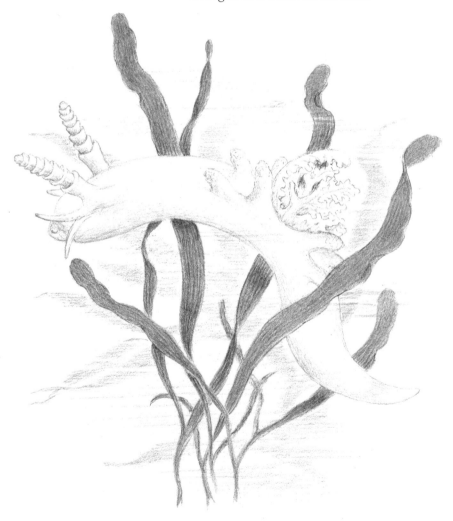

are proof of a common ancestry shared with the shell-bearing types, but all traces of that shell are lost at a very early stage.

Most of the nudibranchs do not have true gills; their respiratory organs are visible on the outside as often bizarre appendages arranged in rows or bunches along the sides. Thus the Dorididae, one of the nudibranch families, have feather- or leaf-like gills arranged in a circle around the anal opening on the back. They usually have a pair of retractile feelers on the back which look like the segmented antennae of insects. Most also have a pair of short tentacles near the mouth.

One of the prettiest of the European members of the family is *Ancula cristata,* a small, milk-white nudibranch with a slender alabaster body, from which the large feelers and the fern-like gills rise like bizarre plants. This vegetarian moves effortlessly and gracefully through the maze of algae on which it lives. It is often found in the company of relatives of the type genus *Doris,* especially the star slugs *Doris pilosa* and *Doris proxima.* They are distinguished by the lack of the anterior pair of tentacles; the leaf-like gills form a rosette on the back.

Attractive as many of them are, the Dorididae cannot compete in beauty of shape or in coloring with their close relatives, the Aeolididae. Most members of this group are small, usually less than an inch long, although a few "giants" attain several times that length. The majority, however, are tiny, and have to be viewed through a magnifying glass in order to appreciate fully the wealth of hues and patterns that distinguish the various species.

Widely distributed in temperate waters is the bushy-backed sea slug *Dendronotus arborescens,* found both in Europe and in North America. A little over an inch long, this light pink snail with its rows of tree- or bushlike appendages rising from the back must be seen to be appreciated.

Nudibranch of the genus Glossodoris *with blossom-like gills.*

Unlike many other members of the family, the bushy-backed sea slug is a vegetarian and likes to climb around in seaweed seeking food, very much like a caterpillar in the foliage of a tree.

One of the most common as well as the largest of the genus *Aeolis* is the plumed sea slug, which may attain a length of over four inches; it occurs on the coasts of both Europe and North America. As with most of its kin, no description can convey a true picture of this snail with its crowded rows of plume-like appendages.

The plumed sea slug is carnivorous; like many of its relatives, it feeds on coelenterates, the group of invertebrates comprising the jellyfish and its relatives. The preferred prey of this particular species are sea anemones; others feed on polyps, corals, and hydras. All of these coelenterates share one common feature: they are equipped with stinging cells called nematocysts, which help them capture and paralyze their own prey. These stinging cells consist of tiny, poison-filled bags attached to hollow, barbed filaments normally coiled inside the cell. A trigger mechanism activated by touch discharges the contents of the cell and injects the paralyzing poison through the hollow filament into the body of the prey.

The stinging cells are not only a means for capturing prey; they are also a powerful defensive weapon. It is interesting to note that the slugs feeding on these invertebrates are obviously quite immune to the coelenterates' poison, which can paralyze

The common plumed sea slug of temperate waters.

animals many times the size of the tiny snails. What really fascinated the first naturalists to examine the slugs under a microscope, however, was the discovery of nematocysts in their dorsal appendages. Since these stinging cells are found nowhere else in the animal kingdom except in the coelenterates, their presence in the snails seemed more than a coincidence, and numerous theories were advanced in attempts to furnish reasonable explanations. In 1858, the English naturalist, T. Wright, came forward with a theory that caused an immediate and heated controversy. He reasoned that the nematocysts swallowed by the snails as they feed upon the coelenterates are not digested; instead, they are stored in the tiny appendices of the snail's intestine that protrude into each gill branch. After having "loaded" the appendages, so to speak, the snail can then use in its own defense the "stolen" nematocysts of its victim!

The nudibranchs on these pages belong to several different genera grouped in the family Aeolididae.

Incredible as the theory sounded, many biologists accepted Wright's premise of "acquired weapons," while others rejected it. New research has confirmed some important points in favor of his explanation, one being the fact that the nematocysts of each snail species are identical with those of its preferred prey species.

Today, the premise that the stinging cells found in the snails are ingested during feeding is accepted as a fact, even though the question of how they remain untouched by the digestive juices of the snail is still unanswered. According to a recent theory, the storage of the stinging cells in the appendages is nothing more than the removal of potentially dangerous substances from the snail's vital organs, and their use as defensive weapons is only a byproduct of that removal. Nonetheless, the entire process is hardly rendered less mysterious by such an explanation.

To the average observer, the truly exquisite patterns, color combinations, and designs that grace the bodies of the small snails are fully as wonderful as their anatomical peculiarities. As the Swiss zoologist, Adolf Portmann, noted, it would take a Parisian fashion expert to dream up proper names for the costumes in which the little gastropods are robed. No description can convey a picture, nor can any photograph or illustration hope to capture the depth and luster of these rich, frequently iridescent hues, where blue is highlighted by silver, pure gold gleams against velvety blacks and browns, and orange-red glows against a background of transparent, shimmering blue-green.

Faced with the wealth of colors and patterns displayed by the aeolid snails, scientists naturally sought an explanation in which some function—*any* function—could be assigned to the patterns. However, as mentioned earlier in connection with

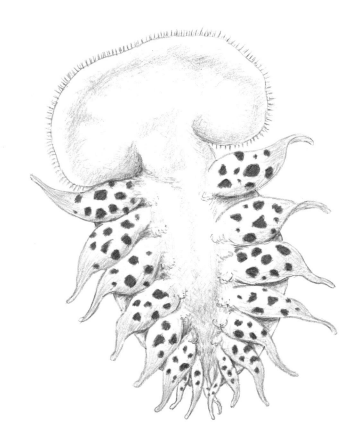

One of the strange snails of the genus Tethys.

shell patterns and colors, there is no satisfactory "functional" explanation for much of the variety of design and color found in the animal world.

The beautiful and the bizarre are found side by side among the nudibranchs; one of the strangest is the veiled snail *Tethys fimbriata* of the Mediterranean Sea. The head of this species broadens into a fringed sail that serves to propel the animal through the water; the rows of fernlike gills add to the weird appearance of this species.

Much more conventionally shaped are the snails of the genus *Elysia;* despite the winglike lobes that extend from both sides of the body, these species look very much like the typical slug. The tapering lobes fulfill the double function of swimming and respiratory organs, for all gill appendages are lacking in this group. Although not brilliantly colored, their rich, subtle, velvety hues are very beautiful. The green velvet snail *Elysia viridis,* which occurs from the Mediterranean to the North Sea, is a fine example of its group. This elegant little gastropod has a head with two short, ear-shaped feelers, and a slender body from which the undulating lobes extend laterally. The color of this snail is a velvety black shading into a rich deep green, and then again into dark brown. This background color is speckled with numerous fine white spots as well as with iridescent green-blue and metallic red dots. As the animal moves along, these colors shift and change with the light angle in a

The green velvet snail Elysia viridis.

rainbow play of color heightened by the dark background. Other snails of this group have similarly attractive color combinations; the nudibranchs have perhaps a greater number of exquisitely colored and bizarre-looking members than any of the other gastropod groups.

The partial review of the snails of land and sea attempted in this book thus comes to an end. It is to be hoped that some idea of the myriad forms and colors and the curious lifestyles found in this large and fascinating group has been conveyed with a measure of success.

Bibliography

Abbott, R. Tucker, *American Seashells*, D. Van Nostrand Co.,
  Princeton, N.J., 1955.

—— *Seashells of North America*, Golden Press, New York,
  1969.

—— *Seashells of the World*, Golden Press, New York, 1962.

Emerson, William K., *Shells*, The Viking Press, New York, 1972.

Morton, J. E., *Mollusca*, Hutchinson University Library, Lon-
  don, 1967.

Portmann, Adolf, *Aufbruch der Lebensforschung*, Rhein-Ver-
  lag, Zuerich, 1965.

—— *Die Tiergestalt*, Verlag Friedrich Reinhardt, Basel, 1960.

—— *Meerestiere und ihre Geheimnisse*, Verlag Friedrich
  Reinhardt, Basel, 1958.

Stix, Hugh and Marguerite, and Abbott, R. Tucker, *The Shell:
  Five Hundred Years of Inspired Design*, Harry N. Abrams,
  New York, 1968.

Glossary

Bivalve

Any mollusk with a two-part hinged shell; also, the shell itself.

Calcareous

Consisting of, or containing, calcite or calcium.

Class

A comprehensive group of animals or plants, ranking below a *phylum* and above an *order*.

Coelenterate

Any member of a group including the corals, sea anemones, and jellyfish.

Crustacean

Any member of a large class of arthropods including lobsters, shrimp, and crabs.

Echinoderm

A marine animal of a group made up of the starfishes, sea urchins, and their allies.

Epiphragm

A thin membranous or calcareous lid with which many gastropods close the shell aperture.

Family

A group of related animals or plants forming a category below the *order* and above the *genus*.

Gastropod

One of a large class of mollusks typically having a univalve shell or no shell at all; a snail or slug.

Genus

A group of related species; a category ranking between the *species* and the *family*.

Hermaphrodite — An individual animal or plant having both male and female reproductive organs.

Mollusk — One of a large group of invertebrates comprising the snails, clams, squids, and their allies, all of which have soft, unsegmented bodies usually protected by a shell.

Nacreous — Pertaining to mother-of-pearl, or *nacre*.

Nematocyst — One of the stinging organs of starfishes, polyps, and other invertebrate marine animals.

Nudibranch — Any of a group of mollusks without a shell in the adult stage, and without true gills.

Operculum — A horny or calcareous lid-like process on the foot of many aquatic snails that serves to close off the shell aperture.

Order — A category below a *class* and above a *family*.

Periostracum — A horny layer covering the exterior of the shells of many mollusks.

Phylum — One of the primary divisions of the animal and plant kingdoms; the *phylum* ranks above the *class*.

Plankton — The minute floating plant and animal life of any body of water.

Proboscis — Any of various tubular processes on the heads of animals; a tubular sucking organ.

Pulmonate — Having lungs or lung-like organs; especially a gastropod mollusk with a lung or respiratory sac.

Radula	A mouthpart typical of gastropod mollusks, consisting of a horny band set with minute teeth.
Siphon	A tubular organ in animals for drawing in or ejecting fluids.
Species	The basic category of plants or animals ranking below a *genus*.
Trematode	Any of a group of flatworms, influding the flukes and their allies.
Univalve	Any mollusk with a one-piece shell; also, the shell itself.
Veliger	A larval mollusk in the stage when it has developed the *velum*.
Velum	The larval swimming organ of many marine gastropods and certain other mollusks.
Whorl	One of the volutions, or turns, of a univalve shell.

Index